WILD
SABAH

WILD SABAH

THE MAGNIFICENT WILDLIFE AND RAINFORESTS OF MALAYSIAN BORNEO

JUNAIDI PAYNE

Photographs by
CEDE PRUDENTE

BEAUFOY BOOKS

First published in the United Kingdom in 2010 by

Beaufoy Books
11 Blenheim Court
316 Woodstock Road
Oxford
Oxfordshire OX2 7NS
UK

www.johnbeaufoy.com

10 9 8 7 6 5 4 3 2 1

ISBN 978-1-906780-11-1

Edited, designed and typeset by D & N Publishing, Baydon, Wiltshire, UK.

Design concept by Behram Kapadia.

Printed and bound in Malaysia by Times Offset (M) Sdn. Bhd.

Contents

PREFACE   7

FOREWORD   9

MAP OF SABAH   10

INTRODUCTION   11

   Origins of Sabah's Name   11

   Land and Climate   12

GEOLOGY AND SOILS   14

   Ancient Rocks   15

   Sabah and Plate Tectonics   16

   Sedimentary Layers   17

   Some Special Geological Features   18

   Geologically Recent Features   20

TREES AND FORESTS   22

   Forest Basics   23

   Sabah's Ever-changing Landscape   25

   How Old are Sabah's Forests?   27

   El Niño Droughts   29

   Individual Trees   30

   Forests of the Coasts and Swampy Plains 31

   Dipterocarp Forests   42

   Montane Forests   46

   Other Forest Types   48

   Other Plants   51

   Sabah's Logging Industry   54

   Sabah's Forests: the Current Situation 62

   Restoring Wild Sabah   64

   Sustainable Forestry in Wild Sabah   71

   Development of Nature Conservation in Sabah 72

Contents

WILDLIFE **76**

    Trees and Wildlife   82

    Primates   90

    Borneo Elephant   96

    Bornean Rhinoceros   99

PEOPLE **102**

    Traditional Human Livelihoods in Wild Sabah   103

    Other Elements of Human Life in Rural Sabah   109

THE REGIONS **114**

    Kota Kinabalu   115

    Islands of the South China Sea   118

    Northern Sabah   121

    West Coast Plains: Klias Peninsula and Tempasuk Plain   126

    Tempasuk Plain   129

    Ulu Padas   130

    Crocker Range and Mount Kinabalu   133

    Interior Sabah: Tambunan to Tenom   140

    The South-east: Maliau Basin and Tawau Hills   141

    Semporna and its Offshore Islands   146

    Lahad Datu: Ulu Segama Malua, Danum Valley and Tabin   152

    Limestone Caves   164

    Kinabatangan Floodplain: Corridor of Life   169

    The Heart of Sabah: Deramakot, Imbak Canyon and Telupid Forest Complex   186

    Sandakan: Sepilok, Offshore Islands, and the Eastern Coastal Wetlands and Kulamba   193

FINAL THOUGHTS   202

GLOSSARY OF MALAY/SABAH WORDS   203

HEART OF BORNEO   203

BIBLIOGRAPHY   204

ACKNOWLEDGEMENTS   205

INDEX   206

Preface

I am pleased to pen a few words for *Wild Sabah*, a book that highlights Sabah's forests and the great biodiversity they harbour. Sabah is indeed a leader in forest conservation, having taken steps to put in place Sustainable Forest Management practices. This has allowed wildlife and plant life to co-exist in our forests, with some of our initiatives drawing wide interest from international organisations.

Fifty-three percent of Sabah's land area is listed as Forest Reserve, State Park or Wildlife Sanctuary, a figure that by global standards is very high. Over the past few years, several additional Forest Reserves have been legislated, steps that ensure all of Sabah's natural forest types are now represented in the State's permanent forest estate, as well as providing a good geographical spread of natural habitats. We are also taking note of on-going studies that suggest the need to relink some of these forest reserves, so that animals can move about from one jungle to another, ensuring their long-term survival.

The Sabah Forestry Department, as the custodian of our forests, has implemented bold strategic initiatives that make a profound and long-term difference to the conservation of the forests of Sabah. The Department deserves credit for making Sabah a shining example of what can be done to maintain an overall goal of sustainable forest management. There is no doubt that as long as the forest management and restoration programmes initiated in recent years are implemented, wildlife and their habitats in Sabah can be sustained, with key sites made accessible for people to enjoy.

I hope this publication will serve as a guide to a wide range of society keen to learn about Sabah and its rich biodiversity, which has become a heritage.

Datuk Seri Panglima Musa Haji Aman
Chief Minister of Sabah

Foreword

The natural vegetation of Sabah is tropical rainforest, represented by a variety of forms, from the coastal mangroves, through dipterocarp forests, to the mountain tops. Only a few years ago, many were of the view that the wood-based industry in Sabah is in terminal decline, and that Sabah's forests were damaged beyond repair. People concerned with conservation and wildlife and wild areas thought that habitat loss and logging spelled the end of biological diversity. We now know that the future is very much brighter, and that the emerging big problem for the world, and therefore for wild Sabah, is likely to be global climate change.

Some of the lowland forests within Sabah's permanent forest estate have indeed been damaged by a history of logging over the past decades, coupled with the adverse effects of two El Niño droughts and fires. A programme to rehabilitate and restore the most significant forests is underway, with emphasis on areas with populations of wild orang-utans and other iconic wildlife species. And there is an array of pristine wild forest areas that remain undisturbed, and that have been designated protected areas for nature conservation.

In *Wild Sabah*, conservation biologist Junaidi Payne and nature photographer Cede Prudente join forces to describe and show in pictures the natural history of wild Sabah. They affirm that a combination of a policy of sustainable forest management, designation of protected areas, and restoration of damaged areas can sustain biological diversity. They also show, uniquely in the equatorial regions of the world, that examples of all of Sabah's natural forest types and a great variety of wild plant and animal species can be seen by anyone with an interest and two or three weeks to spare.

Dato' Seri Tengku Zainal Adlin
President, WWF-Malaysia

OPPOSITE Two special features of Sabah are its sunrises and sunsets, the latter best viewed from Kota Kinabalu across the uninterrupted 1,500km expanse of the South China Sea. Here, sunrise is seen from the peak.

Introduction

With a land area of about 73,619sq km, Sabah represents the northern 10 per cent of the equatorial island of Borneo, the third-largest island in the world (745,000sq km) and home to the largest remaining block of tropical rainforest in Southeast Asia. Borneo is divided between three countries. Seventy per cent of the island is made up of the four Indonesian provinces of East, West, South and Central Kalimantan. Sabah and Sarawak, two states in the federation of Malaysia, are located to the north and west of Kalimantan, while the sultanate of Brunei Darussalam is on the coast not far south of Sabah's southwestern border.

The natural vegetation occurring throughout most of Sabah is tropical evergreen rainforest. These rainforests are characterised by their diversity, with over 10,000 species of plants, perhaps hundreds of thousands of invertebrates such as insects and other small boneless creatures, and about a thousand vertebrate species, including mammals, birds, reptiles and amphibians. In terms of human population, the prehistoric patterns of migration to Sabah and settlement there remain unclear but, as elsewhere in the world, over the last few decades human changes have been much more profound and rapid than in earlier times.

Malaysia, Indonesia, Brunei and the southern Philippines are closely linked ecologically, and before the twentieth century these areas were culturally part of one nexus. Since the 1970s, Sabah has undergone a particularly rapid period of change. Overall, there is now much less forest, especially in the lowlands. This is partly the result of planned conversion of selected natural forests to plantations and other developments, partly caused by El Niño drought and fires in 1982–83 and 1997–98, and partly due to a great increase in the size and spread of the human population. The rapid increase in the human population has occurred both through a rise in the birth rate and internal migration within Sabah by Malaysian citizens, and through immigration from adjacent countries, notably Indonesia and the Philippines.

Throughout Sabah, in many profound ways, the traditional way of life has become a thing of the past. There are now schools and job opportunities in place of subsistence farming, shops and pharmacies have largely replaced the forest as a source of materials, foods and medicines, and most of the population travels via a road network rather than walking or using a boat. But, as we shall see, there remain many truly wild areas in Sabah, as well as some surprises. These include apparently 'wild' areas that were once inhabited by people, and damaged wilderness that can be, and is being, repaired and re-created. An era of massive logging and forest loss is drawing to a close, and land use patterns are stabilising. Wild areas have a greater scarcity value than before, engendering a greater appreciation of the merit of saving them, while nature tourism has had positive impacts by showing that intact forest can have economic value.

Origins of Sabah's Name

There are two main plausible theories regarding the origins of Sabah's name, one from Brunei and the other from the east coast of Sabah. Quite possibly, both contributed to the evolution of the name we use today.

In the earliest known English-language record of the spelling 'Sabah', Sir Hugh Low presented a paper in 1880 based on the *Selesilah* (*Book of Descent*) of the rulers of Brunei, originally written during the 1730s. Low identified Sabah as meaning the Brunei sultan's possessions on the coast to the north of what is now Brunei Darussalam. The next published record of the name came in 1881, in a book by Joseph Hatton entitled *The New Ceylon. Being a Sketch of British North Borneo, or Sabah*. In the will of Sultan Abdul Mumin, who ruled Brunei in the mid-19th century and died in 1885, his northern territories were referred to as '*jajahan sungai sabak*', apparently meaning areas occupied along the northern rivers. Certainly, the region to the north and downstream of the old sultans' palace was what is nowadays the southwestern part of Sabah. Most likely, the term *saba* or *sabak* was used in times gone by in Brunei to refer to 'downstream' and 'northwards' rather than to a particular locality.

An alternative origin of the name comes from the east coast of Sabah, where there is a river named Sabahan. John Hunt, who visited the region that is now the southern Philippines and eastern Sabah around 1811, described Sabahan as a flourishing market centre under the control

Map of Southeast Asia showing the position of Sabah.

of a chief named Datu Sapindin, a nephew of the Sultan of Sulu (the ruler of what is now part of the southern Philippines). The town was inhabited by 1,000 Muslims, who were mostly Bugis (a tribe originating from Sulawesi), together with 800 non-Muslims, and was protected by 45 large guns. William Pryer, the first British North Borneo Company-appointed British Resident of Sandakan, wrote in the 1 October 1886 issue of the *British North Borneo Herald* that 'in Darvel Bay there are the remnants of a tribe which seems to have been much more plentiful in bygone days – the Sabahans'. Indeed, the ancient name for Darvel Bay seems to have been Lok Sabahan (Sabahan Bay).

Further east, on the south side of the Dent Peninsula near the Tabin Wildlife Reserve, is another river, named Sabahat. In an example of the way in which place-names are subject to change, wittingly or otherwise, the Federal Land Development Authority (FELDA) opened up this area for plantations in the mid-1980s, renaming it Sahabat, a Malaysian term for 'friend'.

Land and Climate

About two-thirds of Sabah's land area is regarded as unsuitable for permanent cultivation, based on criteria

The coastline of Darvel Bay, with Mount Silam in the distance at top left. The origin of the name Sabah may lie in an old Brunei word meaning 'northwards' or 'downstream', but equally may derive from the small river and former trading centre of Sabahan, some 13km to the south of this image.

of steep slopes and low soil fertility. Another 11 per cent consists of swamps, nearly half of these freshwater and the balance subject to tidal influence. The extensive tracts of oil-palm plantation that characterise much of eastern Sabah cover less than 20 per cent of the state and are largely situated on the best and most fertile soils.

Average annual rainfall varies from place to place, from 1,800mm in the interior plains to 4,500mm in some mountain ranges. Although there are discernible patterns to rainfall distribution through the year, linked to the globally significant northern and southern monsoons, every year is different. Some years are much drier than the average, while others are much wetter. Periods of very heavy rainfall occur unpredictably and result in localised flooding. Sabahans sometimes refer to the 'rainy season' and 'dry season', but these are really just unpredictable periods of a few weeks or less with daily rain, or with no rain.

In Sabah, as in other regions of tropical rainforest, temperatures vary little through the year. In the lowlands, a very cool night would be 20°C, with daytime highs of up to 37°C in the open. Although it is still too early to be sure, there are indications that Sabah's average temperatures have been increasing since the mid-20th century, and it appears annual rainfall has also increased slightly over previous averages in the first decade of the 21st century.

Even under conditions of undisturbed natural rainforest cover, the combination of heavy rainfall and prevailing slopes renders Sabah susceptible to high levels of soil erosion. The extensive tracts of tidal mangrove swamps along parts of the coastline, especially around the mouths of the large rivers, are a testament to soil particles being washed downstream over the millennia. Most of the sediment is ultimately deposited in the sea, building up as a substrate upon which mangrove seedlings settle and grow.

When the forest cover that represents Sabah's natural vegetation is disturbed to build roads or extract wood, or is removed to make way for plantations and other developments, the already high natural erosion rates increase greatly. Studies carried out in the 1980s and 1990s in a part of the Ulu Segama catchment, for example, showed an overall average annual loss of about 300 tonnes of soil per square kilometre after logging. This rate of loss results in suspended solid concentrations in rivers in excess of 200mg per litre, such that the water requires extensive treatment for human use. The type of long-term land cover most suited to the characteristics of Sabah's geography (high rainfall, soils of limited fertility in most areas, and sloping terrain), combined with the state's growing but sparse human population, is trees. Nature saw to this millions of years ago, and tropical evergreen rainforest was the result. Humans, however, tend to like things that are profitable in the short term, and also more predictable, orderly and easily managed than a tropical rainforest. As a result, oil palms and rubber- and wood-producing trees have replaced much of the natural forest in Sabah. The contest between natural and human forces is still being run in the region. Yet, leaving aside the spectre of climate change, prospects remain good that a fair balance can be achieved in the coming years.

Wild Sabah is characterised by high annual rainfall and, in many areas, steep hills and mountain ranges. The natural vegetation is tropical evergreen rainforest.

Geology and Soils

Ancient Rocks

As part of Borneo, Sabah is also a part of Sundaland, the biogeographical region of Southeast Asia that comprises the islands of Sumatra, Java and Borneo, their surrounding smaller islands, and the undersea shelf of land that connects them to mainland Asia. Underlying Sabah and much of the rest of Borneo are massive slabs of the earth's oceanic plate that were thrust up onto the continental shelf of Southeast Asia during the Triassic period, a time when dinosaurs were starting to spread across the earth elsewhere. Most of these crystalline basement rocks (some of which are more than 200 million years old) lie deep below geologically younger rocks that were subsequently deposited on top, but there are some outcrops along the road from Silam into the Danum Valley.

A prominent feature of Sabah's geology is its ultrabasic, or ultramafic, rocks, which are igneous and derived from the earth's mantle, the layer just beneath the crust. Ultrabasic rocks are characterised by having a very low silica content (whereas most rocks are rich in silica) and low potassium content (a chemical element essential for plant growth), but a very high level of magnesium, iron and other metals. While ultrabasic rocks are dark greyish in colour, the soils that develop from them are a dark chocolate-orange, a reflection of the high iron oxide content. They are also poor in organic matter and micro-organisms,

OPPOSITE Igneous rocks known as ultrabasics form an arc of scattered hills and mountains from northern through to southeastern Sabah, with the most accessible outcrops seen at road cuttings near Telupid and Ranau. Rich in iron, magnesium and heavy metals, the soils derived from these rocks are a dark chocolate-orange colour.

BELOW Most ultrabasic mountains and hill ranges, such as those shown here, have been retained under natural forest. Some plant species are either unique to these mountains or found elsewhere mainly in heath and peat swamp forests.

and tend to become very desiccated during rainless periods. Large mammals such as rhinos and elephants rarely, if ever, venture onto ultrabasic soils, most likely owing to the low productivity of plants here and the odd balance of minerals in the soils and leaves. Ultrabasic outcrops – some small, others massive mountains – occur in an arc stretching from northern Sabah, through the centre around Telupid, and eastwards via the Danum Valley and Mount Silam.

Over many tens of millions of years, the area we now call Sabah remained deep under the sea, where it was slowly covered by showers of microscopic marine protozoa called radiolarians. By this process, much of the original crystalline basement rock became covered in a silica-rich rock called radiolarian chert, most of which in turn was later covered by sediments that eventually formed newer rocks. Only a few outcrops of the chert can be seen in Sabah, along the lower Segama River.

Gold, copper and other metals occur sparsely in Sabah's rocks, with small concentrations in the ancient crystalline basement of the upper Segama River, the middle Labuk River valley, around Mount Kinabalu and on the Semporna Peninsula. The prospect of finding large deposits of these valuable metals was one of the main reasons for the interest of the British North Borneo Company in securing rights over Sabah in the late 19th century, but it became clear within a couple of decades that the deposits were too small and scattered to offer much commercial potential

Sabah and Plate Tectonics

Today, the whole of Borneo island, including Sabah, is relatively stable in geological terms, but for most of the past 60 million years it probably experienced frequent and major changes brought about by movements in the earth's crust. One of the main factors involved was the convergence of three of the 12 tectonic plates that form the earth's surface, the Pacific, Eurasian and Australasian, causing great movements centred on the undersea region to the northeast of Sabah. This, in turn, has at various times caused the area now represented by Sabah to be rotated, lifted and pushed down.

Sedimentary Layers

The process by which Sabah's basement rocks and chert gradually became covered by sediments started tens of millions of years ago, when sediments consisting mainly of fine rock particles and clays were washed in massive quantities off mainland Asia. The rocks they formed include sandstones, mudstones and shales. Much of northern and western Sabah was created in this way during the Eocene and Oligocene epochs, some 20–40 million years ago. The layers of these sedimentary rocks can be seen along road cuttings in many of the hilly and mountainous parts of the state. The sandstones vary in hue from whitish to pale yellow, through orange to maroon, while the mudstones and shales vary from dull brown through greyish to purple-black.

Pulau Berhala, an island at the entrance to Sandakan Bay, is the northernmost example of a series of sandstone layers that were tilted upwards into saucer-shaped basins several million years ago as a result of massive underground collapses.

The process through which Borneo's thick sedimentary rocks were laid down from mainland Asian run-off continued during the Miocene, 10–20 million years ago, bringing with it two geological formations that are distinctive to parts of central and eastern Sabah. Quartz pebbles, visible in curiously scattered piles just below the land surface, can be seen in parts of the Kinabatangan and around Sandakan (including next to the airport). These pebbles, useful nowadays for rural road-building in a region of otherwise rather soft rocks, ended up in their present locations after a long journey, having initially been deposited in ancient estuaries that are now dry land. Even more distinctive and much grander in scale are massive sandstone and shale sequences that were laid down in very shallow coastal waters. In some places these sequences are interlayered with coal, which is the fossilised remains of peat-swamp forest. These layers were periodically deformed by widespread geological movements and massive underground collapses into a series of circular basins, unique to Sabah and visible on satellite images of the region. The largest and most prominent is the Maliau Basin, from where the array

A section of the seven-tiered Maliau Falls, in the heart of the 25km-wide Maliau Basin, the largest such basin derived from massive sagging into softer sediments beneath. Now covered in undisturbed rainforest, Maliau Basin is a major biological conservation area and water catchment protection zone for the upper Kinabatangan River.

continues to the east and northeast, with some prominent basins and others just distinguishable as small sandstone outcrops scattered through the vast oil-palm plantations that dominate this landscape. The basins culminate in the escarpments behind Sandakan town and the distinctive Pulau Berhala, which marks the entrance to Sandakan Bay.

Coal-mining was carried out on Pulau Labuan during the 19th century and at Silimpopon in southeast Sabah until the early 20th century. The Maliau Basin contains the state's most extensive coal deposits. The geologically more recent layers of sedimentary rocks covering Sabah, and surrounding its land mass under the South China and Sulu seas, include not only coal but also petroleum oil and gas. Starting in 1974, exploitation of Sabah's offshore oil and gas has contributed greatly to Malaysia's economy.

Some Special Geological Features

In eastern Sabah, between the Labuk River and the area southwards to the border with Kalimantan, and in a few other localities, including Pulau Tiga off western Sabah, are strange outflows of grey mud that are forced to the surface of the land by trapped methane gas. These so-called mud volcanoes vary in area from a few square metres to more than a hectare. The smectite and illite clays that make up the bulk of the mud-volcano clay are believed to have antibacterial properties, as well as the ability to absorb natural toxins that occur in most rainforest plants. It may be for these reasons that elephants and other large herbivorous wild mammals periodically visit Sabah's mud volcanoes to eat the clay. Mud volcanoes also contain more sodium (in the form of common

salt) than other soils and rocks in Sabah, and so are referred to by wildlife biologists as 'salt licks'. That said, some local natural salt licks visited by wildlife are actually springs of ancient sea water trapped between layers of sandstone.

Mixed with the prevailing thick sedimentary layers that characterise most of Sabah's present-day land surface are various rocks of different origins. Examples include pillow basalts, formed when volcanic lava was extruded into sea water, and limestones, formed sporadically in time and space when marine organisms sank and accumulated over millions of years in shallow sites and large holes in the underlying rocks. One of the most ancient limestones in the region is that at Madai, which formed on top of an ancient underwater mountain.

From time to time over the past tens of millions of years, the surface of the earth has alternately risen and sunk, sometimes on a wide scale, sometimes locally. These major up and down movements contributed to the fantastic folding of the massive sheets of sandstone seen along road cuttings when travelling over the Crocker Range and from Kota Kinabalu to Mount Kinabalu. Ripple marks visible in some of these exposed rocks indicate that they were deposited in turbid conditions, while the great thickness of some of the layers (exceeding 1km) suggests that large areas collapsed from below, leading to very long periods of sediment build-up under the sea.

ABOVE Sabah's geological crowning glory is Mount Kinabalu, which consists of a mass of granite thrust up through ultrabasic and sedimentary layers. The fantastic jagged peaks and troughs of the summit zone are mainly the result of erosion by former ice sheets moving slowly over the mountain top, and alternate freezing and melting of the ice.

LEFT The scenic islands of Bodgaya, Boheydulang and Tetagan, off Semporna, are the remains of the rim of a large volcanic crater. Other remnants of volcanic activity in south-eastern Sabah include parts of the Tawau Hills and Mount Pock on the Semporna Peninsula.

19

The Lipad mud volcano at Tabin Wildlife Reserve is one of the largest of these geological features: outflows of grey salty clays forced to the earth's surface by methane gas. Large mammals visit these sites, probably to immerse their feet and consume the salt and bactericidal and toxin-absorbing clay.

In the Lahad Datu region are conglomerates and breccias, formed as small rocks have become cemented together over geological timespans, and also indicating periods of uplift or slumping of the earth's surface. More localised up and down movements of the earth's surface, some associated with geologically recent volcanic activity, help to explain the odd variations in rock types and hill shapes seen in southeastern Sabah. From the Late Miocene to Quaternary time, up to as recently as about 25,000 years ago, volcanoes were periodically active in the Semporna–Tawau region. Their remnants can be seen in the form of cone-shaped hills and rich brown soils, and the stunning islands of Bodgaya and Bohey-dulang off Semporna, part of what was once a crater rim (see page 146).

Pride of place in Sabah's geology must go to Mount Kinabalu, which rises to 4,095m above sea-level and has a distinctive glaciated granite top, unique in Southeast Asia. The mountain represents a massive intrusion of igneous rock that thrust up from under the earth's crust through the sedimentary Crocker mountain range. The granite centre and top of the mountain, technically called a pluton of monzonite, was originally liquid magma that cooled over a period of about 6 million years to form hard rock. Over that time, the covering and surrounding sedimentary rocks were eroded away, to expose the magnificent granite peaks visible today.

Geologically Recent Features

Some of Sabah's distinctive landforms are of recent geological origin, being less than a million years old. Inland, these include the fertile loamy Tenom soils, derived from erosion of the surrounding hill slopes and famous for producing high-quality coffee and fruits. Smaller areas of similar soils at higher elevation at Tambunan allowed the development of productive rice fields, which in turn gave rise to the distinctive rice and bamboo culture of the

Tambunan Dusuns (see page 133). In contrast, the Sook and Keningau plains, between Tenom and Tambunan, are sandy, gravelly and rather dry, but their extensive flatness, coupled with temperatures that are less oppressive than those of the coastal plains, probably encouraged human settlement from early times.

In the coastal zones are swampy plains, mostly formed over the past 20,000 years or so. On the west side of Sabah, they include peat, mangrove and freshwater swamps. The coastal peat swamps of the Klias Peninsula form the northern fringe of great tracts of peat that stretch southwards through Brunei and Sarawak to West Kalimantan in Indonesia. On the east side of Sabah are extensive coastal mudflats, where the soil is inundated daily with sea water, as well as freshwater swamps in the floodplains of the largest rivers. Patches of exposed dead coral reef can be found on the eastern tip of the Dent Peninsula and also in Kulamba Wildlife Reserve, possibly the remnants of a time about 4,200 years ago when, for a short period, the sea rose by as much as 5m above its current level.

Soils in Sabah tend to be quite rich in clay, more so than those in western and southern Borneo, and this feature is especially pronounced in the east, between Sandakan and southwards to the border with Kalimantan, Indonesia. The presence of abundant clay tends to promote fertility and moisture in the soil. The prevailing heavy rainfall throughout the region, however, tends to leach nutrients downwards, both directly into the ground and downhill from slopes to valley bottoms. Thus, Sabah's alluvial flat lowlands tend to be much more fertile and biologically productive than its hills, mountains and sloping lands. These characteristics became apparent through formal statewide soil surveys carried out in the 1960s and 1970s, which led to the development of a government policy to diversify Sabah's economy away from reliance on timber exports and towards plantation agriculture. Initially, it was thought that rubber, cocoa and rice might form the mainstays of Sabah's east coast agricultural development, but in the event it turned out that oil palm became king.

Much of the eastern coast of Sabah consists of extensive saline mudflats, formed from geologically recent sediments deposited by large rivers, and colonised by mangrove forests and Nipah Palms.

Trees and Forests

Forest Basics

Sabah's natural forests are evergreen tropical rainforests. These are forests of the equatorial regions, where average annual rainfall is usually at least 1,750mm and where there is no pronounced annual dry season. In general, the region's extensive highlands receive the heaviest annual rainfall. Rain may fall at any time of the year, but there tend to be periods when it is especially heavy and frequent, particularly between November and February, during the north monsoon, and between May and August, during the south monsoon. Humidity is very high during these rainy monsoon periods.

Before humans arrived and settled in Sabah, almost the entire land area would have been covered in rainforests. The only exceptions would have been the top of Mount Kinabalu, with its cold, bare rock, and odd patches in the floodplains of large rivers that lie just below sea-level and are covered in water.

Forest plants need five basic requirements to survive, grow and reproduce: sunlight, water, air (primarily for carbon dioxide, which is absorbed to synthesise carbohydrate), minerals, and a basic physical substrate on which to be anchored. In general, all these ingredients are abundant in the tropics, with its hot, sunny, wet and weakly seasonal environment. Substrates are abundant and varied, including not only soils but also tree trunks, branches and leaves, on which lianas, ferns, orchids and mosses can gain anchorage. The abundance of the various ingredients accounts for the bewildering denseness, stature, luxuriousness and exuberance of tropical rainforests, which in Sabah alone contain more than 3,000 tree species.

OPPOSITE Waterfall in Tawai Forest Reserve, near Telupid, in the Heart of Borneo. The forest here is dominated by *Dipterocarpus lowii*, a tree characteristic of the ultrabasic soils that dominate in this area.

BELOW Fallen dipterocarp fruits (*Shorea* species), showing the single seed and wings characteristic of the family of trees known as Dipterocarpaceae, which dominate undisturbed lowland and hill forests in wild Sabah.

Apart from the physical and chemical requirements of tropical rainforest plants, many also require animals to ensure that they can reproduce. Probably the majority of flowering rainforest species, from the tiniest epiphytes to the biggest trees, rely on insects such as bees and moths, or vertebrates such as fruit bats and small birds, for their pollination. Later, the fruits or seeds of many species are dispersed by birds or mammals.

Leaving aside the possibility that global climate change is already affecting tropical areas such as Sabah, plants here can grow almost unconstrained by physical conditions under the prevailing conditions of near-constant moisture and high, stable temperatures. Instead, constraints to growth are chemical and biological. Some soils are very fertile, while others are deficient in the minerals needed for plant growth. The infertile soils tend to be coarse and sandy, in peat swamps, or on higher, steeper lands where nutrients are constantly leached away by rain. The biological constraint is that, everywhere, new plant growth represents food for bacteria, fungi, insects and vertebrates.

On a very simplified level, Sabah's natural forests can be classified into three major and several minor types. The first of the three major types is forest of the coasts and swampy plains, where the land is low, flat and almost always waterlogged, either with sea water, fresh water or a combination of the two. The second is dipterocarp forest, native to most of the land between the non-swampy coastal regions and the mountains, and once Sabah's most widespread and species-rich forest type. The name dipterocarp refers to the Dipterocarpaceae, a family of several hundred tree species that dominates many of Sabah's original rainforests in terms of biomass (amount of wood and leaves), numbers of trees, forest structure and height. The main features of this plant family are that all of its constituent species are trees, with fruits that each contain a single hard nut. In most species, the fruit has between two and five wings or flanges arranged around the nut. The third major type of forest is that of the mountains, where the land is high and steep, and is usually wet but with occasional damaging droughts. Here, mist blocking out sunlight and low temperatures may also constrain growth.

Sabah's Ever-changing Landscape

With our short lifespans, beliefs and familiarity with only a brief time in history, we humans tend to think of nature as static in the absence of our interference. We imagine that a specific piece of nature is wild and natural if it has not been disturbed by humans over the past century or so.

In fact, wild Sabah is always changing. Wild – even in the sense of remote and undisturbed by humans – does not mean stable. Change in nature can be gradual, or it can be quite sudden and brutal. Research at the Danum Valley since 1986 has shown that big changes in the natural forest environment tend to occur as a result of rare and severe weather events, rather than humdrum trends over long periods. A heavy, sustained rainstorm over an entire catchment, for example, can result in a massive flood that scours leaf litter, logs, boulders and soil down an entire river valley, removing blockages, cutting across river bends and sending thousands of tonnes of soil and organic matter down to the sea within a day or so. Heavy rainstorms bring copious water that soaks and percolates through the hills, and so are beneficial in supplying plants with fresh water. But the sudden abundance of water flowing over the land also washes away some of the nutrient-rich humus and thin topsoil upon which plant growth also depends, and a rainstorm may wipe out an entire season of flowers or developing fruits. This, in turn, may serve to cause a local famine for fruit-eating animals, and pass the baton of advantage to a different array of trees, namely those that have built up reserves of nutrients and are able to bear flowers the following year. Occasional strong blasts of wind, typically associated with night-time storms, can topple swaths of tall rainforest trees even in remote areas.

More profound still are the effects of occasional El Niño droughts, which can kill vast numbers of trees, saplings, seedlings and other plants in the space of a few months (see below). The effect is to provide a new playing field for whatever plants remain alive once the rains come. Those species that happen to be widespread, or are able to produce plenty of viable seeds in the year or two following the drought, may come to dominate the forest for the next century. Something along these lines can be seen in the Danum Valley.

Bornean Gibbon seeking ripe fruits in a strangling fig plant. These plants grow from seeds dropped by gibbons and birds in the crowns of tall trees, eventually enclosing the host tree.

Following the initial designation of the Danum Valley as a conservation area within the Sabah Foundation forest concession in 1982, plans were made to establish a field studies centre here. The choice of location of the centre was based mainly on proximity to the nearest major logging road in use at that time. It was only after establishment of the centre that it was discovered that people had lived along the upper Segama and lower Danum river valleys just a few hundred years ago and probably well into the 19th century. The first clue was the presence of pieces of ironwood coffins and fragments of human bones in rock outcrops near the rivers. Next, charcoal was detected in the soils, indicating fire, probably set by people to clear riverside plots for hillside rice fields. Finally, botanists found that the array of trees near the field centre, in terms of species and size, was more reflective of an old secondary forest than a classical primary forest.

LEFT Danum river. Research at Danum Valley field centre has revealed two important things about tropical rainforests: people may have inhabited them long ago, and rare catastrophic events may affect them for centuries.

BELOW Tawau river (similar in size to Danum river) after a brief rainstorm.

Radiocarbon dating of wood beneath the soil of Pinosuk Plateau (the flat grassy area on the far right of the picture) shows that the forest that covered this area until the 1980s developed only in the past few thousand years.

How Old are Sabah's Forests?

It is sometimes said that Borneo's or Malaysia's forests are the oldest in the world. Statements such as this do have a strong element of truth, but they are a simplification of several factors.

Dipterocarp trees originated during the Cretaceous period, some 65–140 million years ago, when flowering plants evolved and diversified globally. This diversification was particularly pronounced in the ancient southern super-continent of Gondwana, which from around 160 million years ago started to split into Antarctica, Australia, New Guinea, New Zealand, Africa, Madagascar, South America and the Indian sub-continent.

There were clearly dipterocarps throughout Asia by the Oligocene period, albeit of different forms and species than exist today. Fossil pollens indicate that the overall distribution of dipterocarp tree species has declined in extent over geological timescales, leaving a concentration and diversification of the family in Borneo, southern Philippines, Sumatra and Peninsular Malaysia. The earliest Borneo record of a still-living genus of dipterocarp, *Dryobalanops*, the *kapur* or camphorwood, comes in the form of pollen dating from the Mid Oligocene, some 30 million years ago.

During the worldwide ice ages that have occurred periodically over the past few hundred thousand years, some of the land areas that were until recently, or still are, covered in tropical rainforest in Asia, Africa and South and Central America were replaced by savannah. In the coldest periods, sea-levels were more than 100m below their current levels as water was trapped as ice and snow, and the global climate in general was both cooler

Fruiting dipterocarp trees in central Sabah. Fossil pollens and other evidence suggests that Sabah's rainforests persisted during the Pleistocene ice ages while many of the forests elsewhere in South-east Asia shrunk as a result of a cooler, more seasonal climate.

and more seasonal. The montane forests of Sabah and elsewhere would have spread down the mountains to much lower levels than we see now. Large tracts of Sundaland that are now under the sea, as well as some of the extreme lowlands and swamps, would have been savannahs inhabited by large mammals such as elephants, rhinos, wild cattle and deer, and predators such as tigers.

Based on a range of evidence, including present-day plant distributions and fossil pollens, as well as the current distribution patterns of termites and leaf monkeys (langurs), some scientists believe that Southeast Asian dipterocarp forests persisted during the coldest times only as scattered 'refugia'. If this theory is true, during the severest times these forests may have remained only in northern and eastern Borneo (Sabah and East Kalimantan), northern and western Sumatra, and the Mentawai

Islands off west Sumatra. At the peak of each ice age, loss of tropical rainforest to savannah conditions was probably most extensive in Africa and America, while in Southeast Asia the greatest extent of savannah would have occupied much of what is now under the South China and Java seas, along with western and southern Borneo, lowland Sumatra and Java. Thus, the forests of Sabah have probably survived continuously as forest far longer than most other remaining tropical rainforests, but only as patches, which spread and recolonised the lowlands and hills only after the end of the last ice age.

The plant species composition at any particular forest site will have changed over the millennia, varying with trends in climate, rainfall patterns and geological changes such as volcanism, as well as through essentially local, random changes. Yet the Oligocene camphorwood pollen suggests that something closely resembling the modern dipterocarp rainforest has been present in Sabah for at least 30 million years. In addition, fossil pollens and plant spores, dating from roughly 20 million years ago and including tree genera from dry lowlands and peat swamps, as well as from mangroves, have been found in mudstone in the Maliau Basin.

If we accept that the prevailing climate around Borneo was cooler and drier as recently as around 12,000 years ago, and that the sea overran at least some of the coastal plains of Sabah only a few thousand years ago, then while some of the state's forest areas may be tens of millions of years old, others existing today can be only a few thousand years old. Wood retrieved from beneath the clay soils of the Pinosuk Plateau on the south side of Mount Kinabalu, for example, was radiocarbon dated at about 8,000 years old. This area is now a golf course and cattle farm, but a diverse, natural montane forest was present here until the 1980s. In contrast, charcoal beneath a lava flow near Tawau, which was under dipterocarp forest until the 1960s, has been dated at 27,000 years old.

El Niño Droughts

The effects of El Niño events are now widely known, although they are sometimes assumed to be linked to global climate change. In fact, there were several major El Niño events that caused droughts and forest fires in Borneo during the late 19th and early 20th centuries. In a study published in 1996, Rory Walsh of Swansea University

It is possible that occasional El Niño droughts, which occurred before the modern era and which result in widespread famine for fruit-eating animals, may have contributed to the oddly patchy distribution of wild orang-utans in Borneo.

described the occurrence of a drought-prone epoch in Sabah between 1877 and 1915, and again in 1968–98, with a period of generally high rainfall separating them. The 1877–78, 1903 and 1915 droughts in Sabah were all longer and more severe than the 1983 drought that brought global attention to the El Niño effect and forest fires in Borneo.

A glimpse of the 1877–1915 drought epoch can be obtained from photos and illustrations of the time, which suggest that the hills at Sandakan and Kota Kinabalu were covered mainly with grass and scattered bushes. Nowadays, the backdrops of both cities are lush tree-covered hills. Walsh and some other scientists believe that the frequency and length of occasional droughts may have significant impacts on the tree species composition of dipterocarp forests. Indeed, this possibility reflects a broader conclusion of much of the research carried out at the Danum Valley since the mid-1980s: that rare catastrophic events such as extremely heavy rainstorms or drought have a much more profound bearing on forest species composition than the daily norms we see for most of the time.

The 1915 El Niño event is believed to have led to the razing of forest that previously covered much of the Sook Plain to the southeast of Keningau. Small patches of that original forest remain, and harbour several rare and unique plants. But the coarse grass and bushes that replaced the burned forest seems 'natural' to the oldest living human residents of Sook. A scientific paper published in 2006 suggested that, based on the narrow genetic base of Sabah's Bornean Orang-utans (*Pongo pygmaeus*), the population had collapsed from a previously very large number to less than 10 per cent of that. The expansion of oil-palm plantations was suggested as one reason for the apparent collapse. In fact, reading British North Borneo newspapers and other pre-Independence literature, it seems that the pattern and numbers of Bornean Orang-utans may not have changed radically over the past century or more. An alternative possibility is that the El Niño droughts in the late 19th and early 20th centuries might have been sufficiently severe so as to cause major mortality of sensitive species of wildlife, which then may need decades or even centuries to rebuild their numbers.

Most of the tall trees visible in this picture are probably between one to three centuries old, but different tree species achieve different ages before a natural death. An old Macaranga Tree will be forty years, while an old Belian Tree may be one thousand.

Individual Trees

At the individual level, mature trees in Sabah's forests can vary in age from a few decades to over a thousand years. Some of the fast-growing species, such as the tree known in Sabah as Laran and in the international timber trade as Kadam or Kadamba (*Anthocephalus chinensis*, also classified as *Neolamarckia cadamba*), and even some of the dipterocarps that have evolved to colonise tree-fall sites, such as *Parashorea tomentella* (a species occurring only in Sabah and East Kalimantan), can become tall, canopy-level trees by 30–40 years of age under good soil and light conditions. The state's 'classic' fast-growing pioneer trees are species of the genus *Macaranga*, which have distinctive three-lobed leaves. By 30–40 years of age, these trees are already old, and start a natural process of dying and collapsing.

The massive, slower-growing species of dipterocarp trees of primary rainforest may be 300 years old or more. A *Shorea superba* tree that fell near the Danum Valley Field Centre in 2001, for example, was estimated by radiocarbon-dating techniques to have started life between 1660 and 1685, making it about 330 years old when it died of natural causes. Beyond around 300 years of age, the cumulative effects of infection by fungi, destruction by termites and loss of branches tends to cause individual trees to become weak and increasingly likely to die, or to be toppled by gusts of wind. An exception is the Borneo Ironwood, also known as Belian (*Eusideroxylon zwageri*), the oldest, densest and hardest tree in Sabah. These trees can live to over a thousand years and produce sawn wood that can last untreated for more than a century, whether used a fenceposts, bridges or piling. Examples of ancient Borneo Ironwoods can be seen at Sepilok.

Forests of the Coasts and Swampy Plains

Coastal and mangrove forests

Along the coasts and on low-lying plains of Sabah, forests are found on swamps and flat lands where water – whether salt, fresh or a combination of the two – is always near the surface. These habitats are often referred to as wetlands, and in Sabah they have abundant sunlight, water and, in most situations, minerals. However, the underlying substrate is soft, poor in oxygen and acidic, due mainly to the presence of sulphates. Although trees produce oxygen by the process of photosynthesis in their leaves, their roots need a constant supply of oxygen for basic metabolic processes. So, tree roots in swamps tend to be shallow, even protruding upwards into the air to absorb extra oxygen.

They neither extend far downwards to extract minerals from the underlying layers, nor become massive enough to provide physical support to large tree trunks above. Thus, forests in the waterlogged coastal regions tend to be rather low in stature, and poor in tree species diversity, dominated by those best adapted to the prevailing conditions.

Coming from the sea, the earliest human colonisers of Sabah, as well as later traders, pirates and explorers, would have been confronted by three types of coastline. At a few scattered sites are rocky promontories, important landmarks for seafarers in days gone by, while at others there are sandy beaches. Several particular tree species are associated with these beaches, most notably Aru, or Casuarina (*Casuarina equisetifolia,* superficially resembling a Christmas tree), and Penaga Laut, or Ball-nut (*Calophyllum inophyllum*).

The third type of coastline, which was and still is the most extensive in Sabah, is a muddy coastline that is periodically inundated with tidal sea water, where mangrove forests, consisting of just a few types of tree, have adapted to grow. All mangrove trees have characteristic aerial or stilt roots, protruding above the substrate on which they grow. Patches of hundreds of hectares of mangrove forest are scattered along the west coast of Sabah, while great tracts of many thousands of hectares dominate the south side of the Klias Peninsula and most of the state's east coast.

In the past, Sabah's mangroves were exploited quite heavily for their wood, which was used mainly as firewood and to make charcoal, as well as for piling and scaffolding. Mangrove-tree bark is rich in tannin, and was used to tan natural-fibre ropes before the advent of plastics. In the early 1970s, licences were granted to allow the clear-felling of large tracts of the state's eastern mangroves for production of mangrove-wood chips, which were exported to Japan to manufacture rayon. Most of the trees felled were of the genera *Rhizophora* and *Bruguiera,* and the industry reduced 70,000ha of mangrove to almost bare mudflats. A decade later, studies

Kulamba Wildlife Reserve, on the north coast of the Dent Peninsula in eastern Sabah. All the tall trees along the coastline behind the driftwood on the sandy beach are Aru, or Casuarina (*Casuarina equisetifolia*).

showed that such drastic felling ran the risk of creating large areas of mudflats on which there was inadequate natural regeneration of trees. At the same time, research by biologists highlighted the fact that mangrove forests form a nursery area for many forms of marine life, and that the economic value of this resource was likely to be greater if left intact for fisheries than if cleared for industrial products. In 1986, the Sabah government stopped the felling of mangroves for woodchip in favour of a conservation regime, whereby most of the state's mangroves would be allowed to regenerate.

Mangrove forests do regenerate by themselves, as long as new seed sources float in with the tides, and – as with the regeneration of any natural system – adequate time is allowed. Along the coastal highway just north of Kota Kinabalu, a sense can be gained of the robustness of mangroves and of the importance of time in restoring natural ecosystems. Over the past few decades, much of the former mangrove forests here have been filled in to create new land for housing. Yet *Lumnitzera* mangrove trees have naturally colonised a lagoon created by the construction of the highway, where fresh and salt water mix.

Long, soft-bodied beetles known as *kelip-kelip*, or fireflies (*Pteroptyx* spp.), are associated with some of the larger mangrove waterways. Their larvae live in wet soil and leaf litter, where they prey on snails and other invertebrates. The more attractive adult fireflies are nocturnal, producing a greenish-yellow light from organs in the abdomen, used in mating displays. When hundreds of fireflies display, clumped on individual trees, one is reminded of Christmas-tree lights. Fireflies may display on a variety of trees in mangroves, as well as on the coppery-leaved Dungun tree, or Looking-glass Mangrove (*Heritiera littoralis*), which occurs in both western and eastern Sabah as scattered individuals growing on higher mud mounds, protruding above the surrounding mangrove canopy; and on the spiny-trunked Apid-apid tree (*Excoecaria indica*), one of the most robust swamp trees, which can be found from the mouth of the Kinabatangan River upstream into freshwater swamps.

Ground view within mangrove forest showing the characteristic stilt roots of *Rhizophora* trees and pencil-like pneumatophores of Avicennia trees. These appendages are permeable to gases and facilitate absorption of oxygen for growth and metabolic processes in the poorly aerated mud.

Long-tailed Macaque (*Macaca fascicularis*) foraging for crabs, fish and molluscs on mudflats.

Among Sabah's larger animals, the Proboscis Monkey (*Nasalis larvatus*) is associated with mangroves, but in fact travellers to this habitat are as likely to see Long-tailed Macaques (*Macaca fascicularis*), which forage on the mudflats for crabs, fish and molluscs, as well as the much rarer and more attractive Silver Leaf Monkey (*Trachypithecus cristatus*) and Estuarine Crocodile (*Crocodylus porosus*). Bornean Orang-utans feed in mangroves where this habitat adjoins transitional and freshwater-swamp forest.

Palm-swamp forests

A special type of mangrove consists of dense stands of the Nipah Palm (*Nypa fruticans*), which grows in clumps where salt water intrudes into freshwater swamps. There are also extensive tracts of Nipah swamp, running to hundreds or even thousands of hectares, where fresh water flows into tidal mudflats. These areas are among the most impenetrable natural habitats to humans. Remarkably, fossilised Nipah Palm pollen and seeds from more than 60 million years ago have been found in scattered places across the world, including northern Europe. These findings indicate that the Nipah is one of the most ancient living flowering plants, and that the climate has changed radically over different parts of the globe since the flowering plants first evolved.

In the past, Nipah Palm fronds were routinely cut to make roofing thatch, as can be seen in old photos of coastal settlements in Borneo and Southeast Asia. In 1924, the administrative government of the British North Borneo Company, then based in Sandakan, opened a small factory at Samawang, between Sandakan and Beluran, producing motor fuel from the sugary sap derived from the stems of Nipah flower clusters. The fuel was said to consist of two-thirds ethanol and one-third diethyl ether. By the factory's third season in the first half of 1926, production of fuel was 13,600 litres and costs had been reduced greatly. However, the company directors ordered the factory to be closed, apparently because production costs still exceeded selling price.

Another form of coastal forest, much less well known and far smaller in extent, is Nibong forest, consisting of stands of the Nibong Palm (*Oncosperma tigillarium*) mixed with other trees or palms. The Nibong Palm tends to grow where soils are always wet but rarely inundated by the sea, and are more sandy and less salty than those

found in Nipah forests. Nibong Palms can grow to a height of 30m, and are sometimes mistaken for old coconut plantations, although they differ in having arrays of long black spines on their trunk. The stem produces a wood that is both strong and durable but also flexible, and with attractive dark and pale flecks.

OPPOSITE ABOVE Pure stands of Nipah Palm, one of the most ancient of all living plant species, abundant in the muddy estuaries of Sabah's major rivers.

OPPOSITE BELOW Nibong (*Oncosperma tigillarium*) Palm forest (foreground), which grows in dense stands on sandy swamps along the north coast of the Dent Peninsula, with Nipah and mangrove forest on the mudflats behind.

BELOW Transitional (mid-distance) and freshwater (foreground) swamp forests at the mouth of the Kinabatangan river. Fire that spread during El Niño droughts has wiped out the tree cover in this area, leaving open swamps with sedges and grasses.

Transitional and freshwater-swamp forests

On the seaward side of the floodplains of Sabah's large rivers, transitional zones occur where mangrove and Nipah forests merge with non-saline swamps and dry land. Traces of these forests occur on the lower parts of the Kinabatangan, Segama, Labuk, Sugut and Padas rivers. Being in the lowlands and near estuaries, these sites have often been converted to agriculture, although this may fail owing to the great difficulties involved in managing periodic saline intrusions. In addition to clearance for agriculture, these transitional forests tend to be wiped out by fires during El Niño droughts, when the normally high water table drops and fire creeps in from sources in adjacent plantations on dry land.

Moving inland from the coastal swamps and away from all salt-water influence, there are four broad types of forest habitat where there is a high water table. This means that the normal level of ground water is around the same as the surface of the ground itself, fluctuating from just below the surface during dry periods to above it during rainy periods and floods.

Freshwater-swamp forests occur on low-lying mineral soils where the land is periodically inundated with fresh water, both from rain and from nearby rivers, and where no peat develops. Examples of these forests occur on the rather more sandy soils of the north side of the Dent Peninsula in eastern Sabah, notably within Kulamba Wildlife Reserve. Where the soils are clay-rich, they tend to be fertile and, if floods are regular and mild, or can be controlled, are excellent for growing paddy rice or oil palm. The natural forests in the lower Kinabatangan area on such soils that do remain are found mainly below Bukit Garam, and represent examples of a forest type that is now very rare. Tree species composition varies from site to site, in part depending on precise soil conditions and in part on chance factors, but usually only a few are dominant in any one place. The more constantly waterlogged the soil is in any one site, the lower the forest canopy and the lower the diversity of tree species. No dipterocarps tend to grow in these swamps, apart from a few species of the genus *Vatica*.

Freshwater-swamp forest is a habitat that was once more widespread in Southeast Asia, but from early times (thousands, or at least hundreds, of years ago) was converted to rice paddies. The ability of certain varieties of rice to grow on flooded land, where only a few specialised tree species can grow, was part of the reason why rice expanded as the major food crop through Southeast Asia. It is unclear why lower Kinabatangan escaped human settlement and conversion to rice fields, although in the 19th century the British administration thought that piracy from the southern Philippines and head-hunting raiders from Kalimantan were the main reasons. More probably, the unpredictable timing and depth of flooding, compared to that generated by the more seasonal rainfall patterns on much of mainland Asia, made rice growing too risky in the high but erratic rainfall zones of Borneo. Furthermore, floodplains are not a stable ecosystem. Slow attrition and redeposition of sediments mean that the river's course changes slowly, while a large flood event can cause rapid change at some localities, especially by cutting through a big bend in the river. Oxbow lakes may be created almost literally overnight, but they may remain under water for centuries before eventually being filled with sediment and pioneer vegetation.

OVERLEAF A tranquil oxbow lake, lower Kinabatangan floodplain.

Riverine and peat-swamp forests

Along Sabah's riverbanks is found riverine or riparian forest, growing on a terrace of alluvial soil and typically 10–100m wide. Here, the tree species composition differs from that in the forest further away from the river, because riverbanks receive the full brunt of water flow, and so are constantly being eroded or deposited. Usually, owing to build-up of silt, the banks are raised higher than the swamps behind. It is this that leads to the different array of plant species, as well as to local variations according to whether a site is stable, being built up further or being eroded. Figs (of the genus *Ficus*, which includes trees and strangling figs) are often prominent on stable riparian forests. Their fruits (botanically known as a syconium, and actually comprising an array of flowers inside a fruit-shaped rind) represent important food sources for wildlife species, which in riverine forests in Sabah include the Proboscis Monkey and Oriental Pied Hornbill (*Anthracoceros albirostris*).

Riverine forest on raised alluvial terraces along Kinabatangan River. The lush grasses in this zone, and the fact that the soil is higher and firmer than in the swamps behind, make riverine forest a favourite habitat and passage-way for wild elephants.

Peat-swamp forests occur on organic soils of semi-decayed vegetation, which have developed on former mangrove areas or freshwater swamps over the past 10,000 years or so. The process of peat formation starts on exposed, wet, acidic soils, where the acidity and lack of oxygen inhibit bacterial decay. Any vegetation that does grow in these conditions decays only partially after death, and builds up over the years to form peat. Under tropical conditions, the process of peat accumulation can be relatively fast. In any particular area, peat soils and forests are relatively young, although the habitat and plant species they contain may be ancient.

There are two types of peat-swamp forest in Sabah. Topogenous peat occurs where dead, falling vegetation becomes trapped in a broad basin of alluvium, and a rather shallow peat layer builds up. The layer is always wet except in very dry periods, and wetter in the middle than at the edges. This type of forest occurs in the floodplains of the Kinabatangan and Sugut rivers on the east side of Sabah, where it merges with freshwater-swamp forest. In the past, a mix of freshwater- and peat-swamp forests seems to have contained higher population densities of Bornean Orang-utans than is found in forests on dry land.

Ombrogenous peat, in contrast, builds up to depths of 20m or more, with the middle part of the system deepest and the outer areas shallowest. Thus, the middle part tends to dry out and is susceptible to fire, while the edges are dampest and typically support forest of tall stature. Ombrogenous peat swamps cover vast areas, mainly on the west and south sides of Borneo island. The northern fringe of this type of peat-swamp forest occurs in the Klias Peninsula of southwestern Sabah.

Dipterocarp Forests

Until large-scale commercial logging and agricultural expansion commenced in Sabah in the 1950s, the most widespread natural vegetation on non-swampy soils from sea-level to altitudes above 1,000m was dipterocarp forest. Unlike many rainforest plant species, whose seeds are dispersed either by animals, floodwaters or wind, most dipterocarps rely on a combination of gravity and wind for seed dispersal. There are more than 180 species of dipterocarp trees in Sabah, representing about 30 per cent of all the world's living species of this family.

Dipterocarp forest is characterised by a tree canopy that is 40–70m tall, with some 'emergent' trees topping even this, and the majority of its large trees belonging to the family Dipterocarpaceae, with some scattered tall trees of the legume family. The tallest documented individual tropical broadleaf tree, anywhere in the world, is a dipterocarp of the species known in Sabah as Seraya Kuning Siput (*Shorea faguetiana*), in the Tawau Hills (see page 22).

The tree species composition of dipterocarp forests varies with geographical location, soil type, slope, altitude and, probably, the frequency of long droughts over the past few centuries. The variety and complexity of factors involved means that it is impossible to present a simple, clear classification or explanation of this forest type. Globally, the greatest diversity of dipterocarps is centred on the rather sandy soils of lowland Sarawak and Brunei. Southwestern Sabah falls at the northern end of the region, but there is little dipterocarp forest left in this part of the state. Viewed on a Borneo-wide scale, eastern Sabah tends to have a somewhat lower diversity of dipterocarps, a tendency possibly linked to clay soils and a history of occasional yet very severe droughts. The great majority of dipterocarp species can be found in the centre and east of Sabah, owing to the great extent of forest and wide variety of soil types in these regions.

Another reason why no satisfactory classification of Sabah's dipterocarp forests exists is because botanists, foresters and zoologists tend to focus on different aspects. For the general naturalist, four types are outlined below, based on the simple single parameter of altitude above sea-level. In reality, however, there are no sharp cut-offs between the types, which change gradually from site to site.

There are also local variants within each type of dipterocarp forest, usually due to peculiarities of soil. For example, the *kapur* (a general local name for trees of the scientific genus *Dryobalanops*), or camphorwood tree, occurs as five species in Sabah. *Dryobalanops lanceolata*, whose species name refers to the tree's spear-shaped leaves, is the most common and widespread, occurring from extreme lowlands into hill dipterocarp forests where there are clay soils on slopes. A common dipterocarp in and around the Danum Valley, it has proven to be a robust and rather fast-growing species, suitable to aid rehabilitation of degraded dipterocarp forests. In contrast, *Dryobalanops aromatica*, whose specific epithet refers to the spicy odour of the tree's camphor-containing resin, and possibly the species that supplied most of the camphor from northern Sabah for export to China in the late 18th to early 19th centuries, occurs in much of western Borneo but is now very rare in Sabah, found on only a few low sandy ridge forests in the western part of the state. *Dryobalanops beccarii* (named after Odoardo Beccari, an Italian botanical explorer of Sarawak in the 19th century), known as Red Kapur, has dark tawny flaky bark, and grows gregariously on flat and gently sloping, leached sandy soils, both near the coast and far inland. Examples of this tree can be seen most readily from the Sandakan–Kota Kinabalu highway, where the road passes through the Ulu Sapa Payau Forest Reserve about 135km out of Sandakan town, and, even more spectacularly, in the Imbak Canyon Conservation Area. The species often has large cavities in its trunk, making it an important nesting tree for hornbills. *Dryobalanops keithii* (named after Harry Keith, the conservator of forests of North Borneo before the Second World War) is rare, occurring only in scattered areas of northeastern Borneo on clay soils near streams. Finally, *D. rappa*, whose species name is taken from the Iban word *kerapa*, meaning 'shallow swamp', and which is commonly known as the Swamp Kapur, occurs mainly on peat swamps and adjacent very sandy soils in western Borneo, including the Klias Forest Reserve.

Lowland dipterocarp forest

In extreme lowland dipterocarp forests, at altitudes of less than about 150m above sea-level, the topography is generally flat or gently sloping, soils are usually fertile and moist, and there are small, winding streams. Trees are not closely packed, and the upper canopy may be rather uneven, with giant legume trees and strangling figs breaking out above. In Sabah, most of this habitat has been lost to human settlements and oil-palm plantations, although examples exist at Sepilok and in the northeastern fringes of the Danum Valley.

RIGHT Mengaris (*Koompassia excelsa*), a distinctive massive tree of the legume family, found mainly in lowland dipterocarp forests, with very pale grey, greenish-tinged smooth bark and knobs on its main branches.

BELOW The Bornean Ground-cuckoo (*Carpococcyx radiatus*), a very rare bird that seems to favour extreme lowland dipterocarp forest adjacent to rivers and freshwater-swamp forest.

Characteristic trees of lowland dipterocarp forests include Mengaris (*Koompassia excelsa*), a distinctive, massive tree with very pale grey, greenish-tinged smooth bark, and is the favourite nesting tree of wild honey bees (*Apis* spp.); several species of *keruing* (*Dipterocarpus* spp.), with corrugated leaves and aromatic oils in the inner bark; Borneo Ironwood, with extremely dense and long-lasting wood, reddish when fresh and black when old; and Merbau (*Intsia palembanica*), excellent for carving, but now extremely rare in Sabah. Characteristic wildlife species include the Black Hornbill (*Anthracoceros malayanus*) and Red Leaf Monkey (*Presbytis rubicunda*). Several species tend to be characteristic of regions where there is a mix of extreme lowland dipterocarp and freshwater-swamp forests; these include the Bornean Ground-cuckoo (*Carpococcyx radiatus*), Wrinkled Hornbill (*Aceros corrrugatus*) and Bornean Orang-utan.

Lowland mixed dipterocarp forest

On the more elevated plains, on low hill ranges and in the valleys of hill ranges, at an altitude of about 150–300m, is lowland mixed dipterocarp forest. This forest tends to have lower population densities of the larger wildlife species than the extreme lowlands, but a greater diversity of plant and animal species overall. The greater diversity is due partly to the fact that this habitat tends to be extensive, incorporating local variations in soil and slope, which tends to favour a greater variety of tree species and, in turn, creates different local habitats for other life forms. A 53ha plot of lowland mixed dipterocarp forest in the Lambir Hills of Sarawak was found to contain almost 1,200 tree species. A similar plot has not been enumerated in Sabah, but botanists would expect to see a similar but slightly lower number.

There are no species truly characteristic of this habitat, which supports plants and animals that can be found from sea-level almost up to lower montane forests. However, some of the more common spectacular animals found here include the Rhinoceros Hornbill (*Buceros rhinoceros*), Helmeted Hornbill (*Rhinoplax vigil*) and Bearded Pig (*Sus barbatus*). Examples of lowland mixed dipterocarp forest can be seen in the Danum Valley and the southern fringes of the Tawau Hills.

Hill dipterocarp forest

In the hill ranges that characterise much of inland Sabah, at altitudes between about 300m and 750m, is hill dipterocarp

forest. A big difference between this forest and that of the lowland zones is that the land on which it grows is almost entirely sloping – only along some ridge tops and valley bottoms is there any flat ground. Plant diversity remains high, but many species common in the lowlands disappear here and a few specialist hill species emerge instead. Animal life is sparse, a feature linked to lower soil fertility, which implies a lower rate of production of edible plant parts. With fewer insects and birds per unit area, forest noise tends to be more subdued than in the lowlands.

Wildlife most likely to be seen or heard in this habitat includes the Great Argus Pheasant (*Argusianus argus*), Bushy-crested Hornbill (*Anorrhinus galeritus*), Bornean Gibbon (*Hylobates muelleri*) and Red Barking Deer (*Muntiacus muntjak*). In some areas, the upper part of this zone and the lower part of the next (highland) zone is where the spectacular and iconic *Rafflesia* flower can be found. Examples of hill dipterocarp forest can be seen at Poring and in the Maliau Basin.

Highland dipterocarp forest

This habitat type occurs at about 750–1,300m above sea-level. Here, the terrain is almost all steep, daytime temperatures are about 4°C cooler than in the lowlands, rainfall is frequent, and the forest is part of a mountain range. In fact, this is a zone intermediate between hill dipterocarp forest and lower montane forest. Highland dipterocarp forest gives way to lower montane forest wherever there are no more dipterocarps, and where the tree canopy becomes markedly lower over a short distance. In the highland dipterocarp zones, most plant and animal species found in the lower elevations have disappeared. Only a few dipterocarp species are present, and trees of the oak and laurel families become more prominent. There may also be conifer trees in this zone.

OPPOSITE ABOVE Male Great Argus Pheasant (*Argusianus argus*), a bird of hill dipterocarp forests, making its distinctive, loud '*wau!*' call, which can be heard from a distance of more than a kilometre across broad valleys.

OPPOSITE BELOW The massive parasitic flower of *Rafflesia keithi* which, like other *Rafflesia* species, occurs mainly in highland dipterocarp forest. It is speculated that the poor soils of the highlands place constant nutrient stress on plants, including the *Tetrastigma* vine, which is parasitized by *Rafflesia*.

Montane Forests

Up in the mountains beyond about 1,000m above sea-level are montane forests. Here, conditions for plant growth are harsher than in the swamps and dry lands at lower elevations. For a start, light levels are lower, because of frequent cloud cover. Water is normally plentiful, because it is up in the mountains that rain falls most frequently and abundantly. However, the incessant flow of water from above flushes nutrients out of the system, into streams and down to the lowlands below. As a result, plants struggle to obtain sufficient minerals, especially those that are naturally rare. And, when there are periodic natural long dry spells, the system is shocked. The extra sunlight on these cloudless days further dries out the plants by evaporating water from the normally wet leaf litter, and then from the very thin, rocky topsoils.

A variety of montane forests occurs in Sabah, of which two major forms can be recognised. Most widespread is lower montane forest, which stretches from below 900m on some mountain ranges to above 2,000m on Mount Kinabalu and other tall peaks. Generally, this forest is dominated by trees of the oak, laurel and myrtle families. There are more than 50 oak species in Sabah,

Highland dipterocarp and lower montane forests in Maliau Basin. These forests contain a few dipterocarps, such as *Shorea laevis* (selangan batu kumus) on lower ridges and *S. platyclados* (seraya bukit) at higher elevations, and numerous species of oaks, chestnuts, laurels, myrtles and conifers, the latter including the genera *Agathis*, *Dacrycarpus*, *Dacrydium*, *Phyllocladus* and *Podocarpus*.

which occur mainly, or only, in lower montane forests above about 1,000m. In some areas, lower montane forest is also rich in tropical conifers. In parts of the Crocker Range, Tawau Hills and Maliau Basin, just one genus of conifer, *Agathis*, dominates, and it may be the largest tree in these forests. In other areas, additional types of conifer occur, including members of the genera *Podocarpus* and *Phyllocladus*.

At altitudes higher than around 2,000m above sea-level, but as low as 1,200m on smaller mountains and exposed ridges, is upper montane forest, also known as cloud, mossy or elfin forest. This consists of stunted bushy trees, less than 17m high, mostly with small leathery leaves. A variety of other plants is also found here, including ferns, liverworts, blankets of mosses, rhododendrons and pitcher plants.

ABOVE At 4,095m (13,435ft) above sea level, Mount Kinabalu is the tallest mountain in Southeast Asia. In between the bare granite top and farms in the foothills there is a variety of natural tropical rainforests, their differences linked to local differences in soil, temperature, light and exposure to wind. After its imposing physical presence, the most prominent feature of Mount Kinabalu is its diverse flora. Many eminent botanists have tried to create a simple classification of Mount Kinabalu's vegetation zones, but this has never really been possible, due in large part to the sheer numbers of species within various plant groups. These range from tiny herbs, ferns and mosses to shrubs, orchids and other epiphytes, and trees. One of the botanical pioneers of Mount Kinabalu, Miss Lilian Gibbs, visited the mountain in 1910. Apart from collecting over 1,000 plant specimens and being the first woman to ascend to the Kinabalu peak, she also made a basic classification of the vegetation types. In 1914, Miss Gibbs listed 203 plant species from Mount Kinabalu, but by 1989 American researcher John Beaman had listed almost 4,000 from the same general area.

LEFT Confined to ultrabasic rocks on Mount Kinabalu and Mount Tambuyukon within Kinabalu Park, the magnificent *Nepenthes rajah* is the king of the pitcher plants. Growing up to 35cm tall and 18cm wide, the pitchers of this species are the largest of all, and are famous for holding up to 3.5 litres of water and for occasionally containing a drowned rat.

47

Other Forest Types

Sabah has three other main forest types that do not fall into those categories described above.

Heath forest

Most common of the remaining forest types, and found in widely scattered sites at all elevations from sea-level to more than 1,000m, are heath forests, known locally as *kerangas*. These occur on infertile sandy soils on flat or very gently sloping terrain. Trees in heath forests are always small – generally about 20m, but often shorter, although some emergents do rise above the canopy – and closely packed, but with sparse crowns. Tree species diversity is low, with very few or no dipterocarps. Under

some heath forests are soils of extreme infertility, consisting simply of coarse white quartz sand with a thin layer of dead leaves on top. A hard iron-rich layer tends to develop in these soils at a depth of about a metre below the surface, a feature that impedes the movement of water, so they tend to become very wet during rainy periods and very dry during rain-free periods. Plants in heath forests tend to have small leathery leaves, a feature associated with conserving scarce water.

On pale yellow sandy soils there are also forests intermediate between heath and dipterocarp, with just a few dipterocarp species of low stature. Both true heath forest and the intermediate form occur in the Sepilok Forest Reserve, beyond the normally accessible areas. A large tract of heath forest also exists in the Maliau Basin,

occupying about 20 per cent of the entire basin surface area at altitudes between 900m and 1,600m. The rather open character of this forest type (which lets in more light) and the plentiful small tree trunks allow growth of a variety of epiphytes and other small plants. In the Maliau Basin heath forest, for example, there are eight species of pitcher plant (*Nepenthes* spp.).

Where sandy heath soils occur in a shallow basin rather than on a slightly convex or sloping land form, the uppermost soil layer tends to be waterlogged for much of the time, and a thin blanket of peat builds up on top. In these areas, the vegetation is sometimes known as *kerapa* forest. This form of heath forest is more common in parts of Kalimantan and Sarawak than in Sabah, but small examples remain east of Nabawan township.

BELOW LEFT Vegetation on a limestone outcrop on the banks of the Kinabatangan River at Sukau. Tree species on limestone tend to consist mainly of some of those found in the surrounding forest, while herbs and shrubs such as begonias and orchids may be of species confined entirely to limestone.

BELOW *Nepenthes veitchii*, one of the eight species of pitcher plants found in Maliau Basin, seen here in 10m tall heath forest at 1,000m altitude.

Limestone forest

Limestone vegetation occurs on the numerous karst outcrops that exist in scattered parts of Sabah, both on the mainland and on Pulau Balambangan and Pulau Banggi to the north. The plant species composition varies with the form of the rock and amount of soil that develops on it, if any. Tree species on limestone tend to consist of some of those found in the surrounding forests, plus a few small-sized species confined to the rock type. Botanists tend to find more of interest in these habitats if they look for the herbs and shrubs. Many limestone outcrops have species of begonia and orchid that are confined to just one or a few outcrops – for example, there are at least two begonias known only from Gomantong. Different limestone outcrops also have different arrays of species of tiny land snails.

Ultrabasic forest

Finally, a distinctive vegetation type occurs on the ultrabasic hills and mountains of Sabah, which is generally more stunted than on soils on similar slopes and altitudes nearby. As on limestone, the tree species found here tend to include some of the array growing in the surrounding forests, along with a few species restricted to ultrabasic soils. The tree composition on such substrates often has similarities to heath and peat-swamp forests, suggesting that ultrabasic soils

Aerial view of heath forest in Maliau Basin, showing the low, even canopy characteristic of this forest type, which is confined to infertile sandy soils.

are similarly infertile for plants. The high levels of magnesium and heavy metals in these rocks, and deficiencies of vital elements such as potassium, nitrogen and phosphorus, do suggest that plants on ultrabasics are stressed by a mineral imbalance. No vertebrate animal species are associated specifically with ultrabasic sites. Indeed, vertebrates exist at very low population densities here, and many species seem unable to secure enough food to be able to sustain breeding populations.

Other Plants

Apart from its diverse variety of native tree species, Sabah has a wide array of other forms of plants. The most prominent non-tree forms of wild plant are probably the strangling figs, of which there are about 30 species, all in the genus *Ficus*. (There are also nearly another hundred species of *Ficus* trees, shrubs, climbers and epiphytes.) Strangling figs start as a small seed, deposited on the branch or trunk of a tree in the faeces of a bird, fruit bat or primate. Initially, they grow slowly, spreading tiny hair-like roots to obtain a hold on their substrate and to glean minerals for growth. Once a few leaves have sprouted, strangling figs may grow rapidly under ideal conditions, such as in the fork of a tree where leaf litter and rainwater accumulate. These figs grow over and around their host tree, sending roots downwards to the ground, and spreading leafy branches that compete with the leaves of the host for sunlight. A few kinds of strangling fig remain small for their entire lifetime, but some reach massive size. For example, the Weeping Fig (*Ficus benjamina*) is a coastal swamp specialist that spreads and towers above the surrounding trees. In dipterocarp forests, old strangling figs eventually overpower the host tree, which dies, leaving the fig as a free-standing plant.

Climbing fig species in lowland dipterocarp forest. Unlike the more prominent strangling figs, which start life from a seed deposited in a tree crown, the rarer climbing figs grow upwards from the ground, like most other woody lianas in Sabah's forests.

Another feature of Sabah's forests, and most especially of its dipterocarp forests, are woody lianas, which are members of numerous plant families. These plants are basically woody stems that grow like a tree as a seedling from the ground, but remain relatively thin and flexible, climbing upwards to drape through the tree canopy. As with trees, some species tend to be specialists of tall, closed-canopy forests, while others are pioneers of open areas. Many liana species provide food for monkeys and apes, and probably also nocturnal mammals, in the form of fruits, flowers and young leaves.

Palms represent a further group of Sabah's flora. Some resemble trees, growing as single trunks with a crown of leaves on top, while others remain as large shrubs overtopped by woody forest trees, and live their entire life under shade. Common in Southeast Asian forests, but also occurring in Australasia and Africa, are the rattans, which are essentially non-woody lianas of the palm family. All rattan species bear spines, which help the plant to gain an attachment to trees, allowing

them to grow upwards towards sunlight and at the same time affording some degree of protection against plant-eating mammals. A few rattan species are harvested, either for traditional local use in making rope, string and baskets, or for the commercial production of furniture.

There are more than 2,000 species of orchid in Sabah. They are found in most forest types, although the bulk of species occur in montane and upper dipterocarp forests, where the air is normally moist. Orchids are rare in lowland forests, except along riversides, but even here they are being depleted through years of collecting. Most orchid species are epiphytes on trees, but a few grow on the ground.

ABOVE Slipper orchid *Paphiopedilum javanicum* var. *virens*, a variety endemic to the Crocker Range in Sabah.

LEFT *Phalaenopsis amabilis*, the Moon Orchid, is another widespread species that grows in tree crowns in the lowlands and hill forests.

Nepenthes, the pitcher plants, are characteristic of very poor soils. The pitcher itself is a device these plants have evolved to capture and digest insects and other small animals, which provide them with nitrogen and other essential minerals that are lacking in very infertile environments. Thus, the 40-plus species of the genus that occur in Sabah are found primarily in montane and heath forests. Their flowers are small and rather inconspicuous.

A variety of non-flowering plants, such as mosses and ferns, may be found in most forest types in Sabah. In general, mosses are most abundant in moist forests at higher altitudes, while ferns occur in many environments, including exposed sites and oil-palm plantations.

Perhaps most famous among Sabah's flora are the three species of *Rafflesia* that occur here, which are actually parasites on vines of the genus *Tetrastigma*. All that is seen of them are the flower buds, which, over a period of many months, grow and blossom into single, large flowers lasting only a very few days. During that flowering time, pollination is carried out by flies and beetles. The resulting fruits are nibbled and eaten by tree shrews and, probably, other small mammals, which disperse the tiny seeds as they run up and down the *Tetrastigma* stems after their meal.

All the plants described so far are native to Sabah, but mention must be made of the acacias, because they are now a prominent feature of parts of the landscape. Introduced to Sabah in the 1960s as potential fast-growing wood producers, acacia trees have spread dramatically, aided in large part by Asian Glossy Starlings (*Aplonis panayensis*), which feed on and disperse their seeds. The acacias (mainly of the species Mangium, or Black Wattle, *Acacia mangium*; and Auri, or Tan Wattle, *A. auriculiformis*) have proven controversial among Sabahans, as thick blankets of these trees have come to dominate roadsides, cuttings, exposed land, landfill sites and most areas where the original native vegetation has been wiped out by brush fire. While travellers on the east side of Sabah will remark on the abundance of oil palms, those on the west coast will – once they have learned to identify them – realise that the commonest trees from Sipitang in the south to Kudat in the north are these two species of acacia and their hybrids.

Nepenthes ampullaria, a pitcher plant species of kerapa forests and peat swamps.

Sabah's Logging Industry

The forests described so far have never, or hardly ever, been disturbed by humans, and are referred to as old-growth, virgin or primary forests.

Commercial cutting of large trees in the coastal lowland forests of Sabah started at the end of the 19th century, using manpower and, later, narrow-gauge railways to bring the logs out of the forest. Thus began a long era of 'logging', whereby selected trees are felled for their timber for local and global markets. Then, as now, logging of natural forests in Sabah does not mean clear-felling of all trees; only some trees are cut and removed. The reason for this is that in any one site there is a variety of tree species, tree sizes and wood qualities. For a start, some species of wood float in water while others sink. And no business can be very efficient if it is producing many different sizes and qualities of product from the same site. Different machines and different methods are needed to cut, transport and process logs of different size and density.

In the early days of logging in Sabah, the pace and environmental impact of the industry was very limited. Massive trees had to be felled with axes, and logs had to be pulled through the forest by men with ropes for loading onto a railway or into a river. Realistically, this could be done only on flat ground or gentle downhill slopes. In the 1950s, two inventions were introduced that would change the face of wild Sabah for ever. The first chainsaw that could be carried and operated by one man was produced in 1950. A few years later, this device was imported to Sabah to fell trees. Powerful tracked machines were brought in at the same time, to make roads by moving earth and rocks, and to pull heavy logs from the forest to these roads. With these machines, almost all terrain, whatever its slope or location, could be reached, and massive logs could be pulled up and down slopes. It was just a matter of time before all forests other than those on the steepest slopes, and other than those designated as protected areas, could be entered.

Aerial view of a commercial logging area, showing logs, hauled from the forest by bulldozers, ready for loading onto trucks that operate on a road built along a river valley. Note that the main logging road is aligned along a low altitude contour, so that construction of the road avoids steep slopes as well as the need to have the trucks operating on steep gradients.

So began an era whereby the combined use of chainsaw and bulldozer allowed centuries-old trees to be cut down and removed easily by small teams of men. Some men specialised in sawing trees down and cutting them into logs, some in operating the bulldozer, some in hooking the logs to a cable that is winched by the bulldozer, some in peeling bark from the logs before their transportation from the forest, and some in maintaining the machines.

Historical perspective

In the 1950s, Sabah's human population and economy were very small. The introduction of chainsaws and bulldozers by a small number of logging licence-holders was merely a more efficient way to do what had been done before the Second World War. The 1960s saw a slow increase in the annual volume of timber cut, as, following independence from Britain and the formation of the federation of Malaysia in 1963, there was an increasing impetus to develop the economy, to improve educational opportunities (the Sabah Foundation was established in 1966 for this main purpose) and to extend the previously rudimentary road network. It was during this period that the most influential people of the day began to realise that they could make great gains for the state, for themselves and for their political parties simply by issuing logging licences and purchasing or leasing bulldozers. In 1970, the strong influence of 12 large forest-concession holders, which dated from the 1950s, was broken, thereby allowing the government greater control over the location and area of forest being logged each year.

In 1973, the recorded cut of timber exceeded 11 million cu m for the first time, up from 6.6 million cu m in 1970. Aside from some fairly minor ups and downs, this level of timber production was maintained annually from 1973 to 1992, and the bulk of the logs were exported unprocessed to Japan. Very roughly, this level of harvesting represents a million ancient trees felled per year, excluding collateral damage to numerous smaller trees surrounding the giants.

From 1992 to 2001, the annual timber volumes cut in Sabah showed a clear overall decline, from around 11 million to 2 million cu m, apart from a small peak in 1997 that coincided with the introduction of a new set of 100-year forest concessions. Since 2001, annual volumes of cut timber have increased again, accounted for mainly

ABOVE Logs, each with a unique number for tracking purposes, are loaded on to trucks for removal from the forest.

OPPOSITE Each logging truck carries between two to about twelve logs, according to log size, per trip.

by the combination of a wave of relogging of logged forest and clearance of remaining trees in areas designated for conversion to industrial tree plantations. Thus, over a period of about four decades, the extensive primary forests of wild Sabah – almost all dipterocarp forests – have been logged and relogged for their timber. Is this sustainable? What does this loss of forest extent and quality mean for the region's biodiversity and for its rare and endangered species?

One internationally used definition of sustainable forest management, agreed upon at the Second Ministerial Conference on the Protection of Forests in Europe in 1993, is 'the stewardship and use of forests and forest lands in a way, and at a rate, that maintains their biodiversity, productivity, regeneration capacity, vitality and their potential to fulfil, now and in the future, relevant ecological, economic and social functions, at local, national, and global levels, and that does not cause damage to other ecosystems'. But before the prospects for sustainable forest management in Sabah can be gauged, we need to know more about the present condition of the logged forests.

Disturbed forests

Sabah's primary forests are now confined to protected reserves and some steep, remote areas. The most extensive habitats in the state are neither primary forests nor plantations, but what are usually called logged forests, meaning forests from which a large proportion of the commercially valuable trees have been removed. These forests are sometimes, incorrectly, called secondary forests, which more properly refers to forest that has grown up after loss of tree cover. For the most part in Sabah, the majority of secondary forests are natural tree regrowth on abandoned hillside rice fields (see 'Rice, rice and rice', page 104).

OPPOSITE Primary and very lightly logged forest (in the background) can be distinguished from logged forest (foreground), from which most of the old, large trees have been removed.

ABOVE Red Giant Flying Squirrels (*Petaurista petaurista*) in regenerating logged forest.

Logged forests vary greatly from place to place in their characteristics. In some places, just a few large trees were removed years ago, whereas in others very little of the original tree canopy remains. In the original primary forests, there is a variety of tree species that are ecologically adapted to conditions of shade, without exposure to full sunlight but with the constant high humidity that exists under full forest cover. Most importantly, the seeds and seedlings of the majority of rainforest plants are suited to such shady, moist conditions. In the absence of human interference, a small percentage of trees in the rainforest die and fall annually, as a result of disease, old age, wind, or large trees falling onto and knocking down smaller ones. This is normal, and creates gaps in the canopy that let in extra light, which in turn stimulates growth of tree seedlings in and around the tree-fall site.

Logging at low intensity, whereby just a few trees are taken from every hectare, mimics these natural conditions. In fact, up to the 1970s, primary forests exploited for timber production were managed under a simple system in which only selected trees of good form, greater than 60cm in diameter, were cut and taken. This system represented a convenient way to obtain timber while enhancing conditions for forest regrowth, as the existing tree seedlings, saplings and immature trees were provided with extra space and light. By the 1980s, the most extensive habitat in Sabah was dipterocarp forest that had been logged once. If left alone, and not affected by fires during droughts, such forests will eventually regenerate.

Ecologically, classic logging at low intensity as described above is quite benign to the forest ecosystem. But the reality is that one has to wait 40–80 years before the forest has recovered and there are sufficient large trees for a second round of logging. Thus, economically, this style and pace of logging became increasingly marginal in the 1970s, once machinery was introduced and global timber markets soared.

Repeated logging, drought and fire

Historically, several factors allowed the second and third logging of already logged forests in Sabah. The need to sustain state revenue in the face of an increasing human population was one such underlying reason. In addition, once-logged forest normally contains good numbers of trees that are large enough to be felled by law, partly because those of lower quality were left behind during the first logging and partly because trees that were too small previously will have grown to adequate diameter to be cut. Thus, a wave of second logging of Sabah's logged forests commenced in the 1980s. Another final major factor was that the land supporting many logged forest areas was allocated for private ownership for the development of plantations in the 1970s and 1980s. In those areas, the entire remaining forests were cleared to make way for these plantations.

However, Sabah's logged forests suffered an additional blow, this one unconnected to industry. It is estimated that around a million hectares of its logged forests were affected by the fires that accompanied the later months of the El Niño drought in early to mid-1983. The specific origin of most of the fires is unknown, but many were started by embers escaping from plantation development and rural villages, as well as careless disposal of cigarette butts. The fires had a devastating effect for two reasons.

First, evergreen tropical rainforest plants are not ecologically adapted to fire, as they have evolved over millions of years to suit conditions of high rainfall and no fire. This is totally unlike forests in some other parts of the world, where native trees have adapted not only to tolerate fire, but to require periodic fires to stimulate germination of their seeds on and in the ground, and to kill weeds. Thus, fire in evergreen tropical rainforests actually wipes out many tree species, including standing trees, seedlings and seeds embedded in the ground. After the fire has died out and the rains have returned, only weedy plant species remain or recolonise the burned areas. Burned forest areas in Sabah are therefore normally distinctive, being populated by a small array of plant species whose seeds have been brought in by wind or birds, plus a few odd tall standing trees that happen to have survived the fire.

A second reason why the 1983 and subsequent forest fires had such devastating effects is that they swept almost entirely through logged forests – the commonest form of forest in Sabah – facilitated by the rather open, dry conditions and plenty of wood residue on the ground from past operations. Fires can move through primary tropical rainforest after very long spells with no rain, but in contrast to logged areas the burn is light and confined mainly to leaf litter and fallen branches.

After 1983, there were several other years when Sabah experienced forest fires towards the end of long dry spells, notably in 1987 and during the early 1990s. In short, forest fires cause extreme and long-lasting damage to the rainforest ecosystem in Sabah. Another El Niño drought in 1997–98 led to fires in about 500,000ha of Sabah's forests. In that case, parts of Kinabatangan Wildlife Sanctuary and even primary forest on the southwestern fringes of Crocker Range Park experienced fire. The worst single impact was the devastation of about 70,000ha of forest between the Sugut and Paitan rivers in northeastern Sabah.

Forest in Ulu Segama Forest Reserve, degraded by logging and then fire during the 1983 El Niño drought. Only a few tall trees remain, while the paucity of tree seed sources and a thick blanket of weeds prevent regeneration of more trees. The method now used to restore forest on such sites is to plant tree seedlings along rows, and undertake a regime of frequent weed cutting along the rows.

Prior to 1987, this part of Kulamba Wildlife Reserve (viewed from inland; the sea is in the distance) was covered in forest, but a fire during a drought in that year burned the shallow peat layer. Fortunately, in this case, the fire had a positive outcome in producing a grassy wetland habitat used by Tembadau (wild cattle).

As a result of the logging that has occurred extensively over Sabah in recent decades, coupled with fire, logged forest is now the most extensive form of land cover in the state, but with a great variation from site to site in terms of the degree of damage. One way to imagine the situation is in terms of two extremes: sites that have been lightly logged once; and sites where logging and fire have entirely, or almost entirely, wiped out all vestiges of the original forest. In the first case, much of the original forest structure remains in place. Most commonly, such sites are 'islands' of just a few hectares or tens of hectares of forest with good structure, and the dipterocarp trees remaining there act as seed sources for surrounding regeneration.

In contrast, few, if any, original large trees remain in heavily logged forest or secondary forest. There are no, or very few, immature dipterocarps or their seedlings. In such areas, a rule of thumb would be that at least 70 per cent of the tree cover now consists of pioneer tree species, or those that are adapted to open conditions with regular strong sunlight. Common pioneers are members of the genera *Macaranga*, *Trema* and *Pterospermum*, as well as the species Binuang (*Octomeles sumatrana*), Laran and Magas (*Duabanga moluccana*). In the worst cases, these sites have few trees and mostly grasses, shrubs and bushes that are cloaked in creeping plants.

61

Sabah's Forests: the Current Situation

It is clear that a large proportion of Sabah's original wild forests have been damaged or lost over the past few decades. At first glance, the situation seems bleak.

Clearly, the trends of the past few decades are not sustainable, at least in terms of rate of exploitation, for several reasons. For a start, much of the former forest lands that produced the large timber volumes of the 1970s to 1990s are now privately owned and under plantations, mainly of oil palm, so do not produce timber. They may, however, start producing timber again in the future, if palm-oil prices stagnate while production costs rise, and if wood prices trend higher.

Second, apart from within protected areas and on some very steep lands, most of the large trees that are more than a century old have been cut. It would take another century or more to regenerate forests dominated by big dipterocarps.

Third, irrespective of the size of individual trees, the rate of removal of wood from the forests has far exceeded the possible rate of regrowth. A very rough rule of thumb is that Sabah's natural forests, once logged, will naturally regenerate about 1–3cu m of commercial wood per hectare per year, if left unmanaged. This figure is not much when compared to the volumes removed in the past. For example, at the first logging of the best primary dipterocarp forests in Sabah, 100cu m or more of tree trunks were removed from each hectare.

Fourth, there are economic and financial limitations to logging. Large volumes of profitable timber could be extracted in the past because there was no investment in growing the wood, only costs incurred in government administration and in cutting wood and trucking it to the coast. The income obtained by the state, by licence-holders and by contractors involved in cutting trees from natural tropical rainforests was a 'windfall', probably below costs if there had been investment in growing the wood. Apart from that, the profitability of managing logged forests for future wood harvests, and even of the simple process of logging, becomes questionable once all the large trees have been removed. For example, the costs of building and maintaining tens or hundreds of kilometres of roads on rugged terrain, under conditions of high rainfall, are high – potentially higher than the value of the timber. The more remote a particular site and the less timber it contains, then the more doubtful are the chances of a profitable venture.

Biodiversity

Logging, in some areas compounded by fire, and the conversion of forests to plantations, have led to a massive loss of biological diversity in terms of genetic variety within many of the wild species found in forest habitats, simply because there are far fewer breeding individuals now than in the past. While it is obvious that there are far fewer dipterocarp trees, there are in turn also fewer orchids, fewer pollinating insects, fewer birds, and so on. Five hundred individuals of any species contain much less genetic diversity than 500,000 individuals,

Giant forest ants (*Camponotus gigas*) are one of many species that survive well in logged forests; they are even found in secondary forests around Kota Kinabalu.

even though the individuals of that species might all look more or less identical. And there is no way to recover such a loss in genetic diversity within human and economic timeframes, because that diversity evolved over geological timescales.

However, on closer consideration of biological diversity, the situation is more positive. Most significantly, there is no evidence of the extinction of any wild species in recent historical times in Sabah, even among the rarest and most specialised of species. At worst, possibly a few plant species confined to the west coast lowland mineral soils might have been lost as a result of deforestation in this zone, but such species – if any – would still occur in neighbouring Brunei. Some endangered species that, a few decades ago, we might have thought doomed by logging, such as rare orchids or the Bornean Orang-utan, still exist as breeding populations in Sabah. Other species, albeit the more robust, pioneer types, are even more abundant in number now. This applies equally to trees, invertebrates and vertebrate animals. The fact is

that some species will always be naturally rare, and that collecting or hunting, as well as El Niño droughts, will generally have worse impacts on such species than logging. Research on vertebrate animals over the past two decades, in Sabah and in other tropical rainforest regions, has shown that almost all species are fairly robust to logging, and that even the sensitive ones can recover their numbers to some extent after the logged forest is left alone.

Sabah's prime biodiversity concern now, therefore, must be to prevent the extinction of any wild species, by ensuring that measures are in place to help sustain the rarest and most threatened ones. One important step, perhaps not always obvious, lies in recognising that most wild species are not big animals, but rather invertebrates, micro-organisms, fungi and plants, and, furthermore, that all these species live and function not in isolation, but in forest ecosystems. In fact, the array of forest reserves and other protected areas in Sabah has remained quite stable over the past 25 years in terms of area and location, and almost all natural habitat types are now represented. In addition, several new forest reserves have been established in recent years specifically to help conserve rare and localised habitats and species. These include Bukit Hampuan on the southeastern slopes of Mount Kinabalu, peat swamp between the Api-api River and Klias Forest Reserve, and *kerangas* forest near Nabawan.

Probably just under 500,000ha of Sabah's forests, representing about 6.5 per cent of the state's total land area and 15 per cent of its forest cover, have never been logged or affected by fire. The bulk of those primary forests are montane, dipterocarp and heath forests, along with forests on ultrabasic soils. Fortunately, these are the forest types that tend to contain most of Sabah's endemic species (those confined to Sabah or Borneo), as well as species most sensitive to disturbance. Thus, the way forward to conserve Sabah's full array of wild species is to continue to protect remaining primary forests and to embark on a programme to restore at least some of the damaged forests.

Most species in wild Sabah are neither trees nor large animals, but small organisms, such as fungi, which function not in isolation but as a part of the forest ecosystem.

Restoring Wild Sabah

Recalling the definition of sustainable forest management, what are the prospects for productivity and regeneration capacity of Sabah's damaged forests? A small, silent revolution has taken place since the 1990s in terms of how we should view and treat forests and forestry in wild Sabah. Indeed, within the Malaysian and entire Southeast Asian regional context, Sabah is at the forefront of practical research and knowledge on how to deal with vast areas of damaged rainforest that seem desolate and unproductive. These efforts have come largely through the vision of Datuk Sam Mannan, Director of the Sabah Forestry Department, Dr Robert Ong, Head of Natural Forest Research in the department, and dedicated staff in the forestry and conservation divisions of the Sabah Foundation. Some elements of the 'revolution' are not really new, but rather an application of knowledge and principles from an older era of forestry. In that earlier era, natural forests and old, mixed-species plantations were managed at a gentle pace, and as a combination of science, art and the experience of knowledgeable individuals who were equally at home in the forest, government offices and a business environment.

Big picture first

Before describing the technical aspects of restoring Sabah's forests, it is necessary to consider the bigger picture. The first consideration is economic and financial: is it feasible to keep and restore forests if this process costs large amounts of money and if no 'product' will come out of the investment?

A conundrum in retaining and restoring forests is who bears the opportunity cost. The Menanggul river forest shown here was about to be converted to oil palm plantation in 1993 before government stepped in to create a wildlife sanctuary. In this case, a wealthy family with thousands of hectares of oil palm elsewhere remained wealthy, and tens of thousands of people now get to enjoy nature in its most tranquil beauty.

Although not explicit in much of the prevailing debate and literature on tropical forests and nature conservation, there are, broadly, two views on dealing with the dilemma of how to save tropical rainforests. One view – which may be thought of as the 'protected area' approach – is that governments need to set aside specific areas for nature conservation, as a moral or national duty, and make sure that those areas remain intact in the long term. Under this view, the forests are treated similarly to human welfare and cultural artefacts, as obligations that have to be addressed, by raising from independent sources the money needed to sustain them. As national parks, state parks, wildlife sanctuaries and other 'protected areas' tend to lie within this category, so areas outside them are essentially abandoned to landowners, the pressures of human population, market forces and other factors over which concerned conservationists have little or no control.

Among the problems with this view are that only rather small percentages of original habitats are saved, so that much biodiversity will be lost eventually, and that human population growth, changing government policies and other factors can, over time, act to whittle down the size of the protected areas. Another issue that has plagued the protected area approach is a divergence of views on whether and how the support of local communities can be harnessed to play a role in the actual retention of areas protected by laws that are not necessarily popular with them. In many cases, protected areas may offer either no significant benefits to local residents, or benefits only to some.

An alternative view – which may be termed the 'payment for environmental services' approach – is that most natural areas will be lost eventually, unless specific sites that need to be saved can produce a sustainable flow of income-generating or other benefits to at least some parts of human society, not necessarily just people living nearby. Among the problems with this view are that the specific sites some may wish to conserve or restore may be capable of providing only small benefits to few people, so that the stronger argument, overall, remains to convert them to a different use, such as oil-palm or wood plantations. Even if an area of natural forest is not potential prime agricultural land, there may still be a good economic argument to convert it to a wood plantation. Barring any major and unpredictable disaster, for any given land area, plantations of closely and regularly spaced, fast-growing tree species will tend to produce more wood, and more regular and sustained income, than managed natural forests. The 'payment for environmental services' approach may also argue convincingly that a restored natural forest is best for the protection of catchments where water is extracted downstream for human use, and as storage of carbon dioxide, but it is rarely clear exactly who should pay whom for retaining that forest.

While some countries have opted simply for the first approach, Sabah has not only embraced both but has already pursued two additional systems – forest management units, and raising funds to restore damaged forests for biodiversity conservation.

The forest at Danum Valley Conservation Area, one of Sabah's prime protected areas, surrounded by a forest management unit (Ulu Segama Malua), which since 2008 has been placed under a sustainable management regime.

Forest management units

Sabah's third alternative approach to saving tropical rainforests may be termed the 'forest management unit' system. Simply put, this is a just a way to divide up forest regions into units that are convenient for management. But this system is also based on the belief that it is erroneous to think that a particular natural forest area has to be used for *either* wood production *or* conservation purposes, *or* that it has to be surrendered for conversion to plantation or alternative land use. It is possible for a single forest area to be managed both to protect biodiversity and to produce wood on a sustainable basis.

The idea of dividing up natural forests very distinctly into either 'protected areas' or 'wood-production forests' became pronounced during the wood-mining era that started around 1970 and is now drawing rapidly to a close. During that time, there was the simple underlying fact that no individual or company had invested in growing the wood in the rainforests. Whether consciously or not, the rainforests were treated as an unmanaged common resource, to be divided up and parcelled out for logging for profit. Today, however, the sorts of issues that concerned many people just a few years ago – such as whether logging licences should be based on land area or timber volume, or whether to log slowly at a fixed annual rate or rapidly to generate capital for alternative investments – have paled into insignificance. The fact of the matter is that global history shows that there will, sooner or later, be a period of overexploitation, to the point of near annihilation, of any untapped natural resource. Resources that in the beginning seem limitless, that never have the need of serious investment in production, and that have changeable arrangements of control will be at the greatest risk of excessive exploitation. Now that the era of overexploitation of Sabah's natural forests is drawing to a close, the damaged forests can at last be managed jointly for purposes of water protection, soil and biodiversity conservation, and wood production.

Some of Sabah's forest management units are looked after by the Sabah Forestry Department, and some are allocated to specific companies under long-term (typically

ABOVE Teak tree plantation.

OPPOSITE PAGE
LEFT Oriental Dwarf Kingfisher (*Ceyx erithacus*), a common species of old growth, logged and secondary forests, which feeds on invertebrates over forest streams and other lightly wooded sites.

RIGHT Male Asian Paradise Flycatcher (*Tersiphone paradisi*), a conspicuous bird seen commonly in logged forests.

90–100-year) licence agreements. This is no different from the management of any other entity, such as a household or a nation. An entity is manageable in the long run only when it has defined boundaries that everyone has to agree to, and specific objectives, plans and people to manage it. The first such licence arrangement was issued in the 1980s to Sabah Forest Industries, a company operating in Sabah near the Sarawak and Kalimantan border, with pulp and paper production as its main objective. Subsequently, mainly in 1997, other long-term licence agreements were made with other companies.

Seen in this light, forest management units are units of the environment, mainly covered in logged forest, and wood is one of the products and services provided. The Sabah forest management unit system has been criticised by some parties, but those criticisms actually refer to long-term licence agreements, not to the forest management unit as a concept. Some long-term licence agreements did fail, usually for one or both of two reasons. One is that hardly any wood was left to extract by the time the agreements were made, so there was no cash-flow from the licensed forest. Second, some units were allocated to former logging licence-holders, rather than to serious investors in the wood-based industry.

An element of the forest management unit system is that the unit – typically 50,000–100,000ha in extent – is divided into compartments, each of which is a few hundred hectares in extent. The boundaries of a compartment are, as far as possible, chosen to be fairly obvious on the ground, without the need for expensive demarcation. Streams, ridge tops and old logging roads make up the majority of the boundary of most compartments. Each compartment is designated with a major function: either water and soil protection, biodiversity conservation, natural wood production, rehabilitation or conversion to wood plantation. Although frowned upon by many conservationists, this last function may help lead to a net saving of tropical rainforests in the longer term (see 'Sustainable Forestry in Wild Sabah', page 71).

Forest restoration methods

Damaged parts of Sabah's forest can be restored or regenerated to natural forest for various purposes and in various ways, but all boil down to two main principles. First, the purpose of restoration at any one site may be to improve biodiversity (perhaps with a focus on some key species, such as the Bornean Orang-utan) or for wood production, or both. Generally, any kind of permanent vegetation cover is good for water protection, and there is rarely a need to restore forest just for this aim alone. Second, the idea is to restore forest structure, with a mix of native tree species, and with a closed canopy that suppresses weeds and mimics the natural forest that once covered most of Sabah.

One of the pioneering projects to restore damaged forest in Sabah was INFAPRO, initiated in 1993 by Innoprise Corporation, the holding and management company for the Sabah Foundation, and the Forests Absorbing Carbon Dioxide Emissions (FACE) Foundation of the Netherlands. As it happens, the programme was one of the world's earliest initiatives to see if damaged tropical rainforests could be improved so as to absorb extra carbon dioxide from the air. Some of the lessons learned through the project can, however, be applied to the restoration of tropical rainforests in general.

The INFAPRO nursery in the Ulu Segama Forest Reserve, near the Danum Valley, has the capacity to produce and stock a million dipterocarp seedlings after a mast fruiting of these trees. Dipterocarps fruit rarely, unpredictably and in rather short seasons, so once a decision has been made to restore a particular damaged forest with dipterocarp seedlings, the single major constraint will tend to be the availability of seeds. Research at Ulu Segama has also shown that for some species, twig cuttings can be treated to produce roots, which can then be planted out in the forest. Experience has shown that the greatest risk of deaths of the seedlings planted out in the damaged forest comes from insufficient rain during the first months after planting – assuming that other factors, such as the capability of the people carrying out the planting, are well controlled. The lesson from this is to maximise the intensity of seedling planting at the beginning of the periods most likely to experience rain, and to halt it during and at the beginning of likely dry spells.

Cutting of weeds and planting tree seedlings will be needed to restore the diversity of trees and bring back structure to this heavily logged forest.

ABOVE LEFT Male (below) and female (above) Rajah Brooke's Birdwing butterflies (*Trogonoptera brookiana*), a species most often seen in open areas in hill forests.

ABOVE RIGHT Male Ruby-cheeked Sunbird (*Anthreptes singalensis*) on climbing bamboo.

BELOW Forest such as this needs no active restoration.

A second finding of recent years is that where the original forest canopy has mostly gone, and the vegetation consists mainly of fast-growing weeds, those weeds will soon cover and strangle tree seedlings, causing them to die. Thus, a large part of the effort towards restoring forest in degraded sites is to remove weeds from around the planted seedlings, as often as necessary. Many of the weeds that strangle tree seedlings and inhibit forest regeneration consist of non-woody creeping plants that grow very fast and blanket other vegetation, at ground level and up into the tops of saplings and small trees. These types of weed dominate sites where logging damage has been excessive and wherever there has been fire in the forest.

Another type of weed that suppresses forest regeneration in less damaged forests is climbing bamboo of the genus *Dinochloa*. These bamboos are native to Sabah but tend to invade and smother trees if too much of the canopy is removed during logging operations. Studies at Deramakot have shown that the bamboo can be almost entirely eliminated by intensive cutting of all growing stems. Although this involves considerable labour to ensure that growing shoots are not inadvertently left uncut, the costs involved per unit area are only about 10 per cent of the total associated with raising, planting and maintaining tree seedlings in the forest. Once the bamboo has been removed, any existing tree seedlings and saplings previously hidden or suppressed by it can take advantage of the new space and better light conditions, and grow upwards to help restore the forest canopy structure.

To conduct effective restoration of damaged forests, extensive areas need to undergo some form of improvement. A key component of forest restoration is to seek and use methods that achieve the desired results but at the lowest cost. One example is to reduce the number of seedlings planted in each hectare. Some of the initial planting in Ulu Segama in the 1990s saw seedlings spaced at just 3m apart, equivalent to over 1,000 seedlings per hectare. A more cost-effective spacing is around 7m, equivalent to about 200 seedlings per hectare.

One of the lessons from the INFAPRO and subsequent restoration projects in Sabah is that the first step in planning restoration of extensive damaged forest areas should be to map the area according to a very few easily distinguishable current vegetation categories, with a different prescription for the improvement for each. Most convenient in Sabah's damaged dipterocarp forests are three categories. The first category consists of sites where the damage from logging is minor, and the forest will regenerate by itself if left alone. For these sites, the most cost-effective treatment is to do nothing. Seedlings of a variety of rarer species can be planted at such sites, as a means to boost tree species diversity, but in order to recover forest structure over larger areas it may be better to focus on the other categories.

The second category consists of sites where some simple improvement, carefully applied, would boost the prospects for forest to regenerate, at relatively low cost. This category covers sites where there are many pioneer trees and some form of tree canopy, but where very few large old trees remain. Cutting climbing bamboo and weedy trees that are blocking sunlight to tree seedlings below, combined with low-intensity planting of dipterocarp seedlings, represents a suitable treatment.

The third category of vegetation consists of sites where most or all the forest structure has gone, and only a few scattered trees remain in a 'sea' of low weedy growth. This category is the most challenging and expensive to restore. The method that has been developed so far is to cut parallel, straight pathways through the thick vegetation at intervals of about 7m, and to plant the seedlings of only the most hardy and robust, light-tolerant, fast-growing tree species. Although the resulting 'forest' is very poor in terms of tree species, which are also clearly in rows, there are several important features to this technique. First, as these tree species are common and produce many seeds annually, the cost of producing vast numbers of seedlings is quite low. Second, it represents an easy and robust method that does not require years of experience or special skills to implement. Third, with periodic cutting of weeds during the first year or two, a high proportion of the planted seedlings survive and, after two years, the majority are at least 2m tall, sufficient to have formed a rudimentary canopy that starts to shade out the weeds beneath. And fourth, after three to four years the young trees are providing habitats for other plants and animals, which start to enter the planted area from adjacent forests. In the long term, as some trees die, as the growth rates vary from site to site, and as seeds brought in by animal dispersers and the wind grow and start to mature, so the clear planting lines used at the beginning of the restoration work will become gradually less clear, and eventually a real forest will have grown up in place of the original low scrub vegetation.

Sustainable Forestry in Wild Sabah

Sabah has a well-established sustainable forest management model in the form of Deramakot Forest Reserve (see 'Deramakot', page 187). This model was brought into operation in the early 1990s but has not been followed elsewhere in Sabah, ultimately for financial reasons. It has been successful at Deramakot because the reserve is accessible, with moderate topography and good soils. Most forest management units are remote, with steep, broken terrain and generally infertile soils for plant growth. In addition, and most importantly, plantations of robust, productive and multi-purpose crops such as oil palm will, when averaged out, normally yield much more profit per hectare than certified wood grown on equivalent land, as is the case at Deramakot. Thus, the Deramakot model is feasible for only a part of the overall area of Sabah's damaged forests. So what is an alternative that will act to sustain forests but produce better profits per hectare?

RIGHT Rhinoceros Hornbill (*Buceros rhinoceros*) and (BELOW) Bornean Orang-utan (*Pongo pygmaeus*), two species that maintain high population densities in Deramakot and other lowland dipterocarp forests managed sustainably to produce timber.

Forest management units have to be financially and ecologically sustainable. Thus, a certain proportion of the forest management unit probably has to be used to produce wood from plantations rather than from restored natural forests. So, for example, 20 per cent of a forest management unit might be allocated for wood plantations, which end up producing 80 per cent of the unit's income over the long term. The balance of natural forest within the unit could either be left to regenerate naturally or restored as a conservation project, and, either way, could be allocated to supplement the overall income through various site-specific means. Those means might be the generation of hydroelectricity; the protection of water quality for intake points downstream, whereby the water users ultimately have to pay for the forest's existence; or the leasing of sites for purposes as varied as quarrying and nature tourism.

To date, restoration of damaged forests has been mainly for conservation purposes. In the Ulu Segama and Malua forest reserves, for example, tree planting and weed cutting was carried out initially to enhance carbon sequestration, and in more recent years to restore habitat for Bornean Orang-utans and other forest-dwelling wildlife species. However, the restoration methods learned from these environmental projects can also be applied to boosting the wood-production rate for future harvesting in those forest compartments allocated for this purpose by natural forest management. The days of harvesting big forest trees that took a hundred years to mature are largely over. A more efficient and financially attractive way to benefit from damaged production forests may be to boost the numbers of fast-growing pioneer trees, and to harvest them perhaps on a cycle of 20 years, a period that allows them to reach a good size for sawing and peeling (for plywood) and removes them just as their growth rate starts to slow down. This sounds rather like making use of natural forests for better financial returns by mimicking plantations. And, indeed, that is what it is in some respects. But the bonus is that the majority of the land will be covered in a mix of native trees for most of the time, offering habitat for ecologically robust species such as large mammals. In the longer term, it is even possible that restoration and management of a mix of native tree species may prove to be less risky, and to yield more wood per hectare per year, than simple monocultures.

Development of Nature Conservation in Sabah

Not so many decades ago in Sabah, old-growth rainforests were the commonest land cover, and the human population was small. Under those circumstances, wilderness and wildlife could, to a large extent, take care of itself. Sabah gained independence from Britain in 1963 through the creation of Malaysia. Under the constitution of Malaysia, land and forests come under the control of state governments, not the federal government.

Sabah has a strong tradition and legal basis that divides land very clearly between either state land (the state owns it but has no specific formal function or management authority), privately owned land (where a title is issued, either in perpetuity on the basis of native customary rights, or for a specific period – commonly 99

years – for planned conversion of natural vegetation to other use), or reserve land (where specific areas may be 'reserved' by law for a specific purpose, which can range from a road to a native community). Once a specific land area is 'reserved', individual titles of ownership cannot normally be granted. Conversely, once land is granted a title, the most likely outcome will be conversion of forest to plantations or other forms of agriculture. The idea that specific land areas can be owned and managed by a 'community' does exist in Sabah law, yet actual community-level ownership and management of forests and land has never been promoted or practised as it is in some other regions, such as Indonesian Borneo (see 'Customary law, land and forests', page 110).

The state's original reserve concept is found in the Land Ordinance, passed by the British North Borneo administration in 1930, but the concept can be extended to cover forest reserves, parks and wildlife sanctuaries. From this, it is clear that the great majority of land and sea areas important for the conservation of forests, wildlife and marine life are owned by government and managed by a specified government authority, and that most will be a kind of reserve legislated under either the Forest Enactment 1968, the Parks Enactment 1984, the Wildlife Conservation Enactment 1997 or the Land Ordinance. (Note that under the Malaysian national constitution, Sabah's land and forests come under state control, so the term 'national park' is normally not used.)

Headquarters of Sabah Forestry Department (Sandakan), which manages over 3.6 million hectares of Sabah's forests.

TAN: KHAZANAH KITA, HARI INI DAN ESOK

There are three major governmental agencies involved in the protection and management of wild Sabah, along with others that play a supplementary role, and several active non-governmental organisations (NGOs). In terms of land area, forest cover, terrestrial biodiversity and conservation of endangered wildlife, the Sabah Forestry Department is the most significant land manager. This department protects and manages all of the state's forest reserves, of which there are seven categories in over 3.6 million ha, equivalent to nearly 49 per cent of Sabah's land area. The forest land area managed by Sabah Parks, meanwhile, is more than 245,000ha, representing 3.3 per cent of Sabah's land, including some on islands. The Sabah Wildlife Department currently manages wild animals throughout the state, along with the 26,000ha Kinabatangan Wildlife Sanctuary.

Major developments of many sorts have occurred throughout Sabah and Malaysia over the past few decades. In tandem with these developments, the Sabah human population has risen from about 654,000 in 1970 to roughly 3.5 million in 2010. Working with the government of Sabah, the British Overseas Development Authority and the government of Canada started to map the geological, soil and timber resources of Sabah in the late 1960s. The 1976 land capability classification maps and recommendations resulting from those surveys presented a highly utilitarian view of natural resources, based on what land use would be most likely to offer the best returns in physical products and profits from exploitation. Five categories of land use were chosen and mapped. Land that was judged to be totally lacking in any exploitation potential was put in category five, 'best suited for conservation'. Apart from the Turtle Islands off Sandakan and a brief mention of the Danum Valley, no measures were proposed in the studies to protect areas for rare or threatened wildlife species. Tawau Hills was the only area recommended to be retained for water protection purposes. It was against this background that most of Sabah's

eastern lowlands were allocated for development of agriculture; that the timber industry, based on the export of logs and wood products from the natural forests, peaked in the 1980s; and that by year 2000, oil-palm plantations had become the most extensive and profitable form of land use in lower and flatter parts of Sabah.

In 1978, Patrick Andau, the new Assistant Chief Game Warden (actually head of a division of the Sabah Forestry Department; his title was a relic of the colonial era), suggested that it was timely that a state-wide faunal survey of Sabah be conducted. The idea was to obtain information on the status of large wildlife species with a view to making recommendations on which were threatened and what might be done to conserve them, in view of the implications of the 1976 land capability classification study. The faunal survey was conducted by the Sabah Forestry Department and WWF-Malaysia (the Malaysian office of the Worldwide Fund for Nature) from 1979 to 1981. Key recommendations in the 1982

report were that protected areas should be established at Tabin (primarily for the Bornean Rhinoceros, *Dicerorhinus sumatrensis harrissoni*), Kulamba (primarily for the Tembadau, or Borneo Banteng, *Bos javanicus lowi*, a subspecies of wild cattle), the Danum Valley (primarily for Bornean Orang-utans) and Gunung Lotung (later named Maliau Basin, as a wilderness area). In 1983, an exercise was conducted by the government to determine the future long-term array of forest reserves and parks, and in 1984 a very significant amendment to the forestry legislation was passed, which basically determined the main elements of the pattern of forest reserves and terrestrial parks we see today.

The early 1980s were a very significant time for laying several foundations for nature conservation in Sabah. The first factor that led to this was that a collaborative relationship developed between the state government and an NGO, namely WWF-Malaysia. That pattern has continued to the present, with a small array of NGOs assisting governmental authorities in research and conservation of wildlife and wild places. A second and related factor was that it became apparent during the 1980s that clear and targeted reasons to conserve specific areas, and recommendations for very specific conservation actions, have a fair chance of successful acceptance by government. In contrast, vague or unrealistic ideas, such as calls to 'save the environment', to stop logging, or to prohibit further conversion of forest to other land use, are unlikely to help preserve wild areas or species.

A third lesson dating from the early 1980s is that logged forests can have significant conservation value, as discussed above. The prevailing wisdom at that time was that all rare animal species need primary rainforests in order to survive, and that only primary forests were worth the effort of conservationists. By the late 1980s, however, it was recognised that most of Sabah's orangutans were living and breeding in logged forests. It is now very clear that even degraded habitats can be revived to support endangered species and eventually, with effort and time, become functioning forest ecosystems again. Later sections of this book will provide examples of how specific areas of logged forests have become wildlife conservation areas of global significance.

Rainforest Discovery Centre at Sepilok, showing the canopy walkway.

Wildlife

Swiss geologist Eduard Wenk summarised a typical view of Sabah's forests in a report on an eight-day visit to Tabin (then a vast tract of wildlife-rich primary rainforest) in November 1937: 'The hardened jungle traveler in British North Borneo will agree that surprises are few. Day after day, week in week out, you see the same monotonous river scenery, walk in the same type of swampy jungle or else climb one of those innumerable low hills only to be disappointed, when you reach the top, that nothing can be seen.' In his unofficial report, published in the *British North Borneo Herald*, the only wildlife he notes as having seen were two small herds of elephants, a very large python, wasps and leeches. In fact, most of Sabah's wildlife consists of insects and other invertebrates. Large animals are rarely seen, partly because numbers naturally are never high, and partly because visibility in the forest extends at best to only a few tens of metres.

Fossils from Sarawak and Sabah show that several species of large animals, including the Javan Rhinoceros (*Rhinoceros sondaicus*), Malayan Tapir (*Tapirus indicus*) and Tiger (*Panthera tigris*), were present in Borneo until only a few thousand years ago. There have long been debates among scientists as to why large animals became extinct in various parts of the world over the past tens of thousands of years, with some favouring hunting by humans as the likely main reason, and others suggesting ecological or climate changes. Almost certainly, both factors played a role in determining the present array of large animals in Sabah. The existence of fossil orangutans contemporary with human hunters over tens of thousands of years at the Niah caves in Sarawak, and the absence of orang-utans from that region in recent historical times, suggests strongly that humans wiped out the species locally, by hunting and eating them. On the other hand, it is difficult to imagine that humans lacking guns could have exterminated both Malayan Tapirs and Tigers over the entire Borneo island, suggesting that the demise of those species may have been linked to natural changes. Most likely, a massive overall decline in lowland forests, including savannah-like vegetation, as sea-levels rose through what is now the South China Sea over the past 20,000 years, resulted in habitats becoming too small in extent and perhaps not optimum for large mammals in ecological terms.

The specific issue limiting numbers of large mammals in closed-canopy rainforests is that – despite the apparent abundance of vegetation – there is not much high-quality plant food at ground level. The production and turnover of those plants is slow, because of the low light intensity and, worse still for herbivorous mammals, rainforest leaves tend to be rather poor in important nutrients but rich in fibre and natural toxic chemicals. Not surprisingly, therefore, the Borneo Elephant (*Elephas maximus borneensis*), deer and the Tembadau appear to achieve higher numbers in Sabah's damaged forests and at forest edges, where there are grasses and other nutritious herbs. Perhaps Tigers died out because the numbers and production of their main prey animals was just not quite sufficient to sustain them. If we follow these arguments further, we can speculate that even the Sumatran Rhinoceros may have difficulty in obtaining the amount and variety of food plants it needs and, if so, its numbers may never have been very high even before hunting pressure led to its near extinction.

LEFT Tabin mud volcano, one of two large outpourings of salty clay in Tabin Wildlife Reserve (see page 20 for the other), situated in the heart of the Reserve and surrounded by a large swath of dipterocarp forest.

RIGHT A ground-level view inside lowland dipterocarp forest – there is not much plant food suitable for large mammals.

Bearded Pig (*Sus barbatus*) at the edge of Lipad mud volcano, Tabin Wildlife Reserve; this pig species has adapted well to logged forests, where it refuges during the daytime heat, emerging during cooler times to feed on fallen palm fruits.

The Bearded Pig is rather different, as it feeds more on fallen fruits, roots and invertebrates. There is literature dating from many decades ago showing that, especially in Sarawak and East Kalimantan, the species used to form massive herds that travelled over distances of many tens, and perhaps hundreds, of kilometres, seeking fallen fruits. Different forest types, and even the same forest type in different regions with different rainfall patterns, do tend to have peaks of fruit production at different times. It is not clear now, with the decline and fragmentation of natural forest cover not only in Sabah but also elsewhere in Borneo, whether those pig migrations were regular or frequent events. What is clear, however, is that the Bearded Pig is an adaptable species. In Tabin, for example, the commonest large mammal today is the Bearded Pig, and a part of the reason for its abundance is that the animals travel into surrounding oil-palm plantations at night and during dull and rainy weather in the daytime, to feed on fallen palm fruits.

The situation with smaller vertebrate animals – for example, civet cats, rodents, primates, birds, reptiles and amphibians – is rather different. The great majority feed on either invertebrates and other small animals, or fruits and seeds, or a combination of both. In Sabah, the largest of these smaller vertebrates are the Sun Bear, or Honey Bear (*Helarctos malayanus*), and the Bornean Clouded Leopard (*Neofelis diardi*), the latter now viewed as a species of Borneo and Sumatra, separate from the mainland Asian Clouded Leopard (*Neofelis nebulosa*). The naturally low numbers and solitary nature of both species make them very hard to study in tropical rainforests. Malaysian biologist Wong Siew Te has shown that Sun Bears feed predominantly on figs, seeds of trees of the oak family and other fruits, and a variety of invertebrates. Unlike Bornean Orang-utans (see below), Sun Bears are not physiologically able to switch their diet to young leaves and tree bark when fruits are scarce. Clearly, this indicates that the survival of wild breeding populations of the species will depend on the continued existence of contiguous large tracts of good-quality forest, ideally with a variety of forest types in one region, to allow the bears to obtain fruits during different times of the year.

Overall, the general picture for vertebrate animals in Sabah's forests is of high diversity, low numbers of individuals of any particular species, and fairly high levels

of endemism (species that occur only in Borneo). There are also a few species that occur only on the islands of Borneo and Sumatra and, in some cases, also a few of the small islands in between, such as the Western Tarsier (*Tarsius bancanus*). Animals endemic to Borneo that occur in Sabah tend to be species associated with mountains, including squirrels, rats, the Bornean Ferret-badger (*Melogale everetti*) and a variety of birds. But there are also some notable endemics that are lowland dwellers, including three species of monkey and the Bay Cat (*Catopuma badia*).

There are very few specialist feeders among the vertebrates. The most obvious examples are the Sunda Flying Lemur (*Galeopterus variegatus*), an odd mammal that seems to specialise to some degree in feeding on tree sap; and some small birds that specialise in feeding on nectar.

TOP LEFT Sun bear, a scarce and threatened species that feeds on fruits and invertebrates.

TOP RIGHT Sunda Flying Lemur or Colugo, a shy, nocturnal distant relative of the primates that feeds on leaves and sap.

LEFT Western Tarsier, a nocturnal primate that feeds on large insects.

Even among invertebrates, the majority appear to have some flexibility in terms of the species on which they feed, even though the general type of food may be quite specialised. For example, bees and pollinating insects take nectar and pollen from a wide variety of tree species, caterpillars are not necessarily restricted to feeding on the leaves of a single plant species, and invertebrates that dwell and feed in leaf litter may be found in different forest types and even in some mature tree plantations. More extreme specialists include leeches and mosquitoes, which require vertebrate animal blood.

These observations do not, however, mean that all of the estimated hundreds of thousands of species of invertebrates in Sabah are safe from extinction. There is likely to be a decline in species numbers in the coming years,

LEFT Red Leaf Monkey (*Presbytis rubicunda*), a leaf and seed eating monkey found only in Borneo. This species is one of the few larger mammals that seems to decline in logged forests, and is most readily seen in the primary forests of Danum Valley, Sepilok and Tawau Hills.

BELOW Reticulated python (*Python reticulatus*), Sabah's largest snake, a non-venomous constrictor, which occurs mainly in or near damp areas, lowlands and rivers.

OPPOSITE PAGE
ABOVE Two young male Borneo Elephants.

BELOW Little Spiderhunter (*Arachnothera longirostra*), a pollinator of wild gingers.

whether or not the impacts of global warming start to affect tropical rainforests significantly. One reason is that, within any particular group of invertebrates, and indeed any lifeform, there are always some species that have a degree of specialisation and are therefore naturally rare. These may be species that are especially sensitive to dry periods, or that have a narrower array of foods than others. They are the ones most likely to become extinct first in any periods of stress. From a more global view, years of empirical evidence show that the larger an area of natural habitat, the more species it contains, while the smaller the area of the same habitat type, the fewer species can be maintained. If – as in the case of Sabah – there were very extensive areas of natural forest until recent times, and that forest is now fragmented into separate pieces, there will be a lag period, as the largest animals and the most sensitive species gradually fall in numbers towards eventual local extinction.

Trees and Wildlife

With a few exceptions, wildlife in Sabah has to be adapted to life in forests. At any one forest location in the state, there are typically several hundreds of species of trees, which achieve different sizes, shapes and textures when mature, as well as supporting lianas, rattans, mosses, lichens and other epiphytes. To a large degree, it is the complex structure of the forest, as much as the diversity of plant species, that accounts for the diversity of animal life it supports.

One feature common to a number of Sabah's vertebrates is the ability to fly or glide. Of course, all of the state's bird and bat species can fly, and with more than 400 resident species of the former and over 90 of the latter, these groups display a very high species diversity for a relatively limited overall land area. More noteworthy, however, is that the ability to glide between trees has evolved in mammals (the flying squirrels and Sunda Flying Lemur), reptiles (the gliding lizards and even a snake) and amphibians (flying frogs). This feature is linked not only to the fact that the forest contains closely packed vertical supports (trees), between which the animals can glide, but also that gliding uses less energy than walking or flying, and that gliders can avoid predators and parasites that live on the ground.

A gliding female Sunda Flying Lemur (*Galeopterus variegatus*, also known as *Cynocephalus variegatus*) with infant on her belly.

ABOVE The Red Giant Flying Squirrel (*Petaurista petaurista*), the largest of Sabah's flying squirrel species, can glide 70m between trees. It can be distinguished at night from the superficially similar Flying Lemur by its long, thick tail, free of the gliding membrane.

RIGHT Flying Lizard (*Draco cornutus*), which uses its wings to glide for distances of over 10m between tree trunks in the lowland forests of Sabah. Only females descend to the ground, to lay eggs in the soil.

Among other animals, there is a wide variety of associations with trees. There are frogs that spend much of their time in small pools of water in tree hollows. There are lizards that seek refuge in cracks in tree trunks. And there are 16 non-gliding squirrel species that live almost entirely in trees, as well as three species of ground squirrels that still depend indirectly on trees for fallen fruits and refuges in buttresses and roots.

ABOVE Female Orange-backed Woodpecker (*Reinwardtipicus validus* also known as *Chrysocolaptes validus*), a species that forages in pairs or small groups in most forest types.

OPPOSITE ABOVE Indigo Flycatcher (*Eumyias indigo*, also known as *Muscicapa indigo*), one of over 30 flycatcher species recorded in Sabah, and an inhabitant of lower montane forests.

OPPOSITE BELOW Male Red-naped Trogon (*Harpactes kasumba*), a species that favours shaded spots in a wide range of lowland and hill forests on dry land.

Among birds, many species tend to inhabit certain parts of the forest ecosystem, depending on particular features of forest structure rather than on tree species. For example, many babblers live near ground level in tree falls and scrub patches, while trogons and flycatchers tend to favour shady parts of smaller trees, and barbets stay in the tree canopy. Sabah's 18 species of woodpecker all rely on damaged or dying trees of any species as sources of their invertebrate foods. Hornbills need trees for breeding because they make their nests in holes in tree trunks. The most sensitive hornbill species seems to be the Helmeted Hornbill, which tends to decline and even die out in damaged forests. The emerging picture is that, to achieve stable breeding populations, the Helmeted Hornbill may need extensive primary forests with plenty of large old trees. To date, the other hornbills seem more tolerant of forest disturbance, but it is impossible to predict the long-term trends in populations of any species after logging, especially the long-lived species.

Among invertebrates, probably the majority of species are dependent on trees, for living space, for their leaves as a food source, for hunting other insect species as prey, or for obtaining nectar from flowers. Some termite species and beetle larvae feed on decaying wood.

The forest floor is covered in the fallen products of trees, most notably dead leaves, twigs and branches, which provide food and shelter for invertebrates ranging from springtails to mites and millipedes, as well as fungi. More seasonally, vast proportions – indeed, probably the great majority – of the flowers and fruits borne by trees fall to the forest floor and never achieve their evolved function of producing seeds. Once fallen, these flowers and fruits are consumed by insects such as beetle larvae, as well as pigs, deer and fungi. Prominent birds of the forest floor include pheasants, which feed on fruits and insects, and pittas, which feed on invertebrates. Fallen trees, trunks and large branches are often hollow, having toppled as a result of long-term fungal or termite infection. Peer into these hollow trunks and you usually see nothing, but occasionally there may be a snake, mouse-deer, porcupine or even Sun Bear cubs sheltering within.

OPPOSITE Malaysian Tarantula (*Cyriopagopus thorelli*) an arboreal species that after moult is a beautiful grey blue colour. It is found in Sabah and Peninsular Malaysia.

BELOW AND OVERLEAF LEFT Fungi form a vital component of the forest ecosystem, breaking down dead wood and other vegetation to chemically simpler compounds, which can be used by the fungi, and released for absorption by growing trees and other plants.

OVERLEAF RIGHT Ants represent another ubiquitous but often unseen form of life that recycles nutrients in the forest ecosystem; here, ants move a dead cockchafer to their nest.

Primates

The grouping of mammals to which humans belong, known as primates, represents one of Sabah's special wildlife features in terms of number of species (ten, not counting humans) and their variety (apes, monkeys and prosimians). Although there now exists much information on these species, most continue to present some mysteries.

Starting with the Bornean Orang-utan, we still don't know why it is that there are vast areas of seemingly suitable orang-utan habitat in Sabah without orang-utans, and why breeding populations of the species survive in damaged and even very degraded forests. Some possible answers to these questions were outlined above in the previous chapter, and more insights are presented in the chapter describing Sabah's various regions. In summary, however, the answers seem to be roughly as follows. Bornean Orang-utans have evolved to feed primarily on fruits, yet, unlike other fruit specialists in Sabah's forests, such as pigeons, hornbills and fruit bats, which can fly, individual orang-utans are unable to move over large distances quickly to seek food sources during periods of very little fruit availability in their normal home range.

In many regions and forest types, especially hill dipterocarp forests, montane forests, forest on ultrabasic rocks and heath forests, there are only rare and quite short periods of dense fruit production by trees. For the remainder of the time, orang-utan foods hardly exist in these forests. In Sabah's forests, wild fruits are produced frequently throughout the year in only two situations: on the most fertile, moist soils, which tend to be found in extreme lowland dipterocarp forests and freshwater-swamp forests; and where there are several distinct forest types with different times of fruit production, all in close proximity. Furthermore, fruit production is linked not so much to whether a forest is primary or logged, but to the local array of soil types. Logged forests on fertile soils will always tend to produce more fruits than primary forests on infertile soils. Orang-utans do not survive on fruits alone, however. If they did, the species would probably have gone extinct in the distant past. The sub-species of Bornean Orang-utan in Sabah (*Pongo pygmaeus morio*) appears to have evolved the ability to subsist to a large extent on young leaves and bark, especially of pioneer and secondary-growth plants, and other miscellaneous foods for periods of several months whenever there is little fruit available.

The interval between births for wild mother orang-utans is among the longest for all animals – typically six years or more – and only one infant is born at a time. This is likely to be an adaptation to the fact that orang-utans live by intelligence more than instinct, and have to spend an extended learning period with their mother, as well as the fact that a mother orang-utan can cope with only one child at a time in the forest canopy environment. However, these features also make orang-utans extremely vulnerable to hunting. Even low-intensity, prolonged hunting pressure in one region can lead to a situation where orang-utan death rate exceeds birth rate. Not surprisingly, there are regions in Borneo where native people exterminated the Bornean Orang-utan even before the arrival of firearms, even though local conditions of soils and forest habitats may have been suitable for the species.

The Bornean Gibbon, a species endemic to the island and classed as a 'lesser ape', presents a different picture. Gibbons are very unusual among mammals in that their society consists of monogamous family groups, with a single mature male, a single mature female and, usually, two youngsters at any one time. Although recent studies suggest that gibbon society and relationships are not always quite so clear cut as this (just as in human societies), it is the general picture for all evergreen tropical rainforest gibbon populations. Many studies have shown that the family group lives in a territory, which it defends by making loud calls – as an advertisement and warning – and, very occasionally, fighting with adjacent families. Each Bornean Gibbon family territory consists of 25–50ha, much smaller than a typical individual Bornean Orang-utan home range. Most likely, it is simply impossible for a gibbon family to patrol and defend a bigger territory and, being much smaller than orang-utans, they can find enough food year-round in such a small area.

Like other orang-utans, the sub-species of the Bornean Orang-utan found in Sabah (*Pongo pygmaeus morio*) has evolved to feed primarily on a variety of fruits, but this sub-species can subsist for several months on a diet composed mainly of leaves and bark. This is one of the reasons why orang-utans in Sabah can maintain their numbers in logged lowland forests.

There are two species of macaque monkey in Sabah. The Long-tailed Macaque tends to be a specialist of riversides and coastal swamps, while the Pig-tailed Macaque (*Macaca nemestrina*) is more of a dipterocarp forest species. Both are adaptable, however, and can be found on forest edges adjoining plantations.

In addition, Sabah has three species of leaf monkey, also known as langurs. All three feed predominantly on the seeds (but not juicy fruits) and young leaves of trees and lianas. The Red Leaf Monkey and Grey (or Hose's) Leaf Monkey (*Presbytis hosei*) are both dipterocarp forest specialists (although they may extend their range into other, adjacent forest types and even into some tree plantations) that favour plants of the legume family as food. They tend to live in small 'harem' groups, each consisting of one mature male, two to four mature females, and their offspring. Ecologically, these two species seem very similar, and one or the other always dominates in numbers in any particular forest area. The Silver Leaf Monkey,

in contrast, is very much a specialist of coastal areas and the banks of large rivers, and at a glance can be confused with the Long-tailed Macaque, which shares these habitats. The Silver Leaf Monkey is, however, larger and rarer than the Long-tailed Macaque, and lives in smaller groups. Around Abai, in the swamp forests at the mouth of the Kinabatangan River, a reddish-coloured variety (or 'phase') of the Silver Leaf Monkey occurs, which is sometimes mistaken for the Red Leaf Monkey.

OPPOSITE Grey Leaf Monkey (*Presbytis hosei*), a rare primate, which is locally common in Tabin Wildlife Reserve, lives in small harem groups of one male, and two to four females and their offspring.

BELOW Like other gibbon species, the Bornean Gibbon (*Hylobates muelleri*), a species endemic to the island, is unusual among mammals in that individuals live within monogamous family groups. Each group lives in a 25–50ha territory, defended from others by the female's morning loud calls.

Male Pig-tailed Macaque (*Macaca nemestrina*), a species that lives in large groups, often along the boundary of forest and plantations, is often seen at Tabin Wildlife Reserve.

Biologically related to the leaf monkeys is the Proboscis Monkey, which is unique to the island of Borneo. It is estimated that about 6,000 individuals live in Sabah, more than in any other part of Borneo, and within the state the largest population occurs along the lower Kinabatangan River. The Proboscis Monkey is most famed for its nose, but it is also peculiar in several other ways. Weighing about 20kg, adult males are twice as heavy as adult females, an extreme difference between the sexes that is very rare among mammals. The male has a big pot-belly and massive, bulbous nose. The coloration of the male is unique, with its dull orange 'jacket', grey 'tights' and white 'underpants'. Females have a more subdued coloration and a much smaller, snub nose. Unlike Bornean Gibbons and leaf monkeys, which defend territories that hardly overlap, Proboscis Monkeys live in groups in ranges that overlap one another.

Like leaf monkeys, Proboscis Monkeys feed on leaves, seeds, shoots and stems, which occur in abundance wherever there are forests. But the species is almost entirely confined to forests near large water bodies – in other words, coastal mangroves and riverine forests inland. Seeking in vain for ecological reasons why this species might be restricted to waterside forests, most biologists are resigned to a rather weird default explanation. It is clear that Proboscis Monkey society is one where adult males compete with each other to secure a harem of

Male Proboscis Monkey (*Nasalis larvatus*) jumping between two trees. This monkey lives in large harem groups consisting of one male, and many females and their offspring, and as groups of only adult males. The reason for their fixed habit of living near open water and congregating at the water's edge overnight remains a mystery.

females. Thus, any group of Proboscis Monkeys consists either of a single mature male with many females and their children, or of mature and adolescent males that band together. The male that leads a harem group presumably gets to that position by physical strength and stamina, fighting off rivals when necessary. But physical fights are rare. Instead, the male of a harem group constantly has to show off his superiority by displaying his strength to potential rival males. This means a daily display, visible to rival males, of his presence, large nose and

virility. Barring any new ecological information or theory as to why Proboscis Monkeys congregate at the water's edge every evening, it would seem that such a location enables the harem male to show off his dominance to rival males. If that is correct, then the Proboscis Monkey may be a relic of the Pleistocene savannahs, and the water's edge a substitute for the forest and grassland edge where the species' ancestors evolved.

All the monkeys and apes described above are active in the daytime. In contrast, Sabah's two remaining primate species – both prosimians, like Madagascan lemurs and African bush-babies – are active at night. Both are small and range from ground level up into the tree canopy. The Western Tarsier appears to feed primarily on large insects, while the Borneo Slow Loris (*Nycticebu coucang menagensis*) has a broader diet that includes fruits and small invertebrates. Much less is known of the ecology and society of these species than of the monkeys and apes.

Finally, there are a small number of people, including scientists and local residents, who believe that there remains an unidentified ground-dwelling primate in Sabah. This belief is based either on finding strange primate-like footprints in soft soil, or on glimpses of something similar to, but different from, an orang-utan or gibbon either walking on the ground, or very low in the forest canopy. A similar story exists in the foothills of the Kerinci Range in Sumatra. But even there, after years of intensive searching, as well as of reliable reports of people hearing strange and unidentified animal calls, no definite evidence of such a primate has been found. In the absence of any firm evidence – even a hair – nothing more can be said. Perhaps the most likely explanation is that, occasionally, both Bornean Orang-utans and Bornean Gibbons may be born deformed in such a way that allows them to survive and live a solitary existence on the ground, but never breed.

Borneo Elephant

In his 1862 book *Life in the Forests of the Far East*, Spenser St John, the British Consul to Brunei in the mid-19th century, stated that Kinabatangan was the only part of Borneo where elephant ivory formed an important article of trade. Fortunately, that trade has long since stopped, apart from very occasional cases of poaching. When pioneer American wildlife film-makers Martin and Osa Johnson made their first trip to North Borneo in 1920, they photographed a herd of elephants near Sandakan, which in part prompted them to return in 1935–36 to Kinabatangan. Despite the fact that most of the original rainforest of the lower Kinabatangan has since been opened up by roads and converted to oil-palm plantations, an estimated 200 or so wild elephants still live here, moving between forest patches from the river-mouth swamps up to the village of Batu Putih near the Sandakan–Lahad Datu highway. This remnant population probably represents the most concentrated grouping of wild Asian Elephants anywhere, in terms of individuals per square kilometre of land.

Herd of Borneo Elephants on a bank of the Kinabatangan River.

Borneo Elephants in the lower Kinabatangan seem to thrive in grassy areas, forest edges and secondary growth. Dr Waidi Sinun, Head of Conservation and Environment for the Sabah Foundation, who has been visiting the Danum Valley repeatedly over a period of more than two decades, notes that the frequency of sightings of elephants along the road through the logged forests of Ulu Segama has increased significantly over the years. Within the primary forests of the Danum Valley and Tabin, wild elephants live and travel alone or in groups of less than 10 individuals, whereas in open areas of the Kinabatangan and Segama catchments, herds of about a hundred elephants may be seen from time to time. It seems as if the Borneo Elephant is not well adapted to Bornean forests. And therein lies a tale.

The origin of the Borneo Elephant has been the subject of debate since the early European exploration of the region. Based on contemporary 19th-century narratives, and on the peculiar distribution of the sub-species in Borneo, where it is restricted to 5 per cent of the island, it was commonly believed that the elephant is not native. Some zoologists felt that the sub-species might be restricted to fertile lowland soils and natural mineral sources, rare throughout the sandy soils and swamps that characterise much of Borneo, and totally absent in the central hill ranges. A scientific paper published in 2003, based on comparison of DNA among elephants throughout Asia, showed that the Borneo Elephant is related to the sub-species occurring in Sumatra and Peninsular Malaysia, but is significantly different, to the extent that the Bornean population might have been isolated for a period of 300,000 years. The Borneo Elephant appears to be slightly smaller than other sub-species of the Asian Elephant, and a high percentage of the individuals seen in Sabah are immature, so they appear rather cute. As a result, it has also been dubbed the Borneo Pygmy Elephant.

An elephant at Kinabatangan takes a snack of Tangkol (*Ficus racemosa*) figs. These riverside fig trees are important food sources for primates, hornbills and fruit bats.

In 2008, a further paper was published on the subject, highlighting the fact that there were feral elephants on the Jolo Islands in the southern Philippines up until the early 19th century, but no fossils of a Borneo Elephant have been found in Borneo. (Bones of an elephant were uncovered in 1987 from a swamp near the city of Banjarmasin at the southern tip of Borneo, but they seem very recent in geological terms, and are the size of a bull Indian Elephant rather than a Borneo Elephant; presumably these represent the remains of an Indian Elephant sent as a gift some centuries ago to the Banjar sultan.) These observations tend to support an old Jolo legend that Borneo's elephants originated as a gift from a ruler of Java in the late 14th century to the sultan of the southern Philippines. If true, the Borneo Elephant would be the the Java Elephant (sometimes known as *Elephas hysudrindicus*), now extinct, and represents the first – albeit unintended – human preservation of an endangered wild species by translocation to a safer habitat. Does this mean that the Borneo Elephant, possibly not native, is of less importance to conserve than definite native species such as the Bornean Rhinoceros? Not at all. Any large, threatened animal species deserves attention, wherever it happens to be. At present, there are over 1,500 elephants in Sabah – almost as many as in all of Indonesia, and more than in Peninsular Malaysia and several of the mainland Southeast Asian countries. Sabah is, in fact, a major stronghold of the Asian Elephant.

Bornean Rhinoceros

The Bornean Rhinoceros (*Dicerorhinus sumatrensis harrissoni*) a strict forest-dwelling species that feeds almost entirely on the mature leaves and twigs of a wide variety of woody saplings, seedlings and small trees. Its low ratio of body surface area to volume in Sabah's humid tropical conditions probably means it struggles not to overheat. Unlike elephants, rhinos cannot squirt water over their body to cool off, and they do not have large ears or other organs to flap and release heat into the air. Their sole means of trying to stay cool are to travel and feed mainly at night, to stay under tree cover, and to immerse themselves in mud wallows during the hottest middle hours of the day.

Fossils show that the Bornean Rhinoceros has been on the island for many thousands of years and, towards the end of the last ice age, individuals were up to 40 per cent larger than they are today. Scientifically, it is considered to be a sub-species of the Sumatran Rhinoceros, also known as the Asian Two-horned Rhinoceros (*Dicerorhinus sumatrensis*), which was once widespread throughout the forests of Southeast Asia. The species has suffered a never-ending decline in range and numbers over the past few centuries, a trend that continues to the present day. Although habitat loss has played a large role in

this decline, and there is a possibility that only certain forests or soils can sustain breeding populations, the greatest single cause has been relentless hunting for its horns, which are used in traditional Chinese medicine. At the time of writing, the global Sumatran Rhinoceros population was less than 200 individuals, with no more than 40 members of the Bornean sub-species in Sabah and perhaps a few doomed stragglers elsewhere on the

island. The Bornean Rhinoceros is one of the world's most endangered mammals, and possibly now *the* most endangered of all. Without human intervention, this animal will become extinct. The only remaining hope is to promote breeding by actively bringing together into one protected forest site some of the last few fertile females and males. If any Sabah wildlife species needs sustained help to prevent extinction, it is this one.

The Bornean Rhinoceros (*Dicerorhinus sumatrensis harrissoni*) is a forest-dwelling species that feeds mainly on mature leaves and twigs of a wide variety of woody saplings, seedlings and small trees. Its low ratio of body surface area to volume in Sabah's humid tropical conditions probably means it struggles not to overheat. Rhinos cannot squirt water over their bodies to cool off like elephants, and they do not have large ears or organs to flap and release heat into the air.

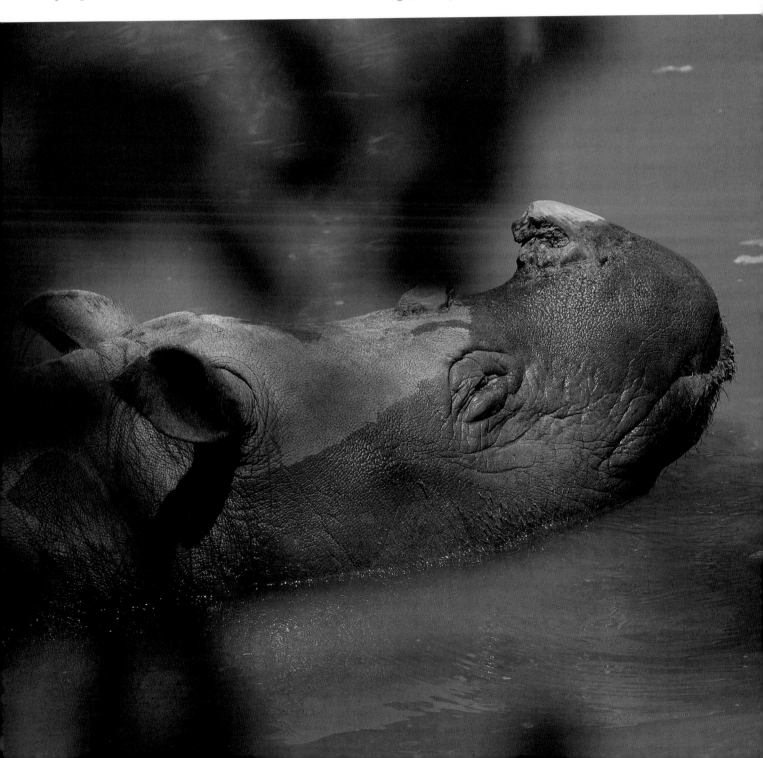

People

Traditional Human Livelihoods in Wild Sabah

A romantic image persists that Bornean native people live in palm-thatch huts or longhouses in the forest, dressed in loincloths and emblazoned with tattoos, hunting with blowpipes. Probably none of that is true now, and the image applied only to a minority of the population even a century or two ago. In Sabah, large palm-thatch huts were made mainly either by seaside-dwelling Bajau people as residences, or by inland people as temporary bases for guarding rice fields. Longhouses and tattoos were traditional in Sabah only among Muruts in the southwestern hill ranges and Rungus people in the far north around Kudat. Imported black cloth trousers, skirts and shirts were already in use when the British arrived in northern Borneo in the late 19th century.

OPPOSITE Traditional clothing and adornments of the Murut people of south-western Sabah include local forest products, such as tree bark jacket, split and dyed rattan hat with feathers of Argus Pheasant, and beads imported by traders.

BELOW Nipah Palm thatch house of the Bajau people of Semporna, built on mangrove poles in the sea.

Evergreen tropical rainforest in Borneo produces very little in the way of plant foods edible to humans, and even those (mainly palms) are seasonal and scattered. In the absence of metal tools, it is likely that the early human inhabitants of Borneo would have relied on starch from the stems of wild palms, tubers and roots, as well as fish, molluscs and other animal life for their food. As a consequence, ancient human communities in Sabah must have been small, scattered and mobile over many thousands of years. The trend by which nomadic hunter-gatherers in Borneo settled as farmers probably started with the introduction of metal tools, possibly less than 2,000 years ago.

Traditionally, most indigenous people of Sabah did not live in the high mountains but on the coastal plains and in the valleys of the major hill ranges. There is hardly any food in the mountains for human hunter-gatherers, while farming opportunities are limited there by steep slopes, prevailing infertile soils, mist and heavy rainfall. There are only two prominent exceptions to this general avoidance of mountain-living. First, there are the Lun Dayeh people, who have grown irrigated rice in flat valleys of the upper Padas River near the Sarawak and Kalimantan border area for hundreds of years. Second, commercial cultivation of temperate vegetables by local Dusun people began in the 1960s in the highlands between Mount Kinabalu and Crocker Range, but this is a business that requires imported fertilisers and roads to markets.

Historically, some coastal communities were predominantly traders. But for most traditional rural societies in Sabah, food production for the family was the main occupation. Apart from hunter-gatherers, who have been absent from Sabah in recorded historical times, and sago-growers in the southwestern swamps of the state, who are predominantly of the Bisaya ethnic group, most communities preferred, and still prefer, rice as a crop, a plant introduced from mainland Asia.

Rice, rice and rice

Rice plants need full exposure to the sun in order to grow, so rice production is incompatible with forest cover. On flat coastal lands, and in broader highland valleys where dykes can be constructed, irrigated rice can be grown in flooded fields. Four to six months are needed from planting to harvest, and yields are high. Where dykes cannot be built on slopes, or can be but are subject to flood damage, non-irrigated rice is planted alongside other edible plant crops on land cleared of tree cover. This is known as swidden farming, whereby rain is the sole source of water, and where most fields are left fallow for most of the time.

The preparation of dry-land fields for planting rice seeds (felling and chopping standing vegetation, drying and burning) may take three to four months, depending on rainfall patterns, and another five months are needed from planting to harvest. Traditionally, field preparation was mainly a task for men, while planting and harvesting might involve any able men and women, and guarding the growing rice and ripening grain was mainly a job for children and old folk. Yields of rice grains from such rain-reliant farm fields can reach 300kg per hectare or more, but may be much lower, depending on rainfall, soil fertility and damage by insects and wildlife.

A dry-land rice field may be used for just one, or up to a maximum of two, successive annual crops, before it becomes swamped by weeds, and then a period of years is needed for soil fertility to recover and for the weeds to be suppressed and eliminated by natural regrowth of tree cover. On fertile soils, a few years are adequate for the fallow period, while on infertile slopes 20 years or more are needed before an old dry-land rice field can be used again to grow rice. Where human population pressure is high on poor soils, farmers are forced to return to fields too soon, and trees are gradually lost to grasses and shrubs. In these circumstances, there is a continuous battle against weeds, and rice yields may be low. To minimise the risk that land and forest will be overstressed, even a small, traditional swidden farming community in rural Sabah typically needs at least a few hundred hectares of farmland, plus another few thousand hectares of adjacent forest land to supply wood, meat and other forest products.

There is a wide spectrum of situations among rural swidden farming communities, from remote locations where the system has been stable for a long period, to sites near logging roads where this kind of farming is carried on in previously remote sites and motivated in part by a desire to claim land as well as to produce food. In between these extremes, traditional communities have for generations adapted to changing circumstances, improving rice yields through trial and error, and growing alternative crops such as corn or rubber on former rice fields. This variation in farming styles is

Irrigated rice fields on the western coastal plain of Sabah. Rice (grain) is the traditional staple food for most ethnic groups in Sabah. Rice plants need full exposure to the sun in order to grow, so rice production is incompatible with forest cover. On flat coastal lands, and in broader highland valleys, irrigated rice can be grown in flooded fields, as seen here. Irrigated rice fields are successful only on clay-rich soils, which retain water, but much of Sabah's west coast is sandy or peaty, while the flood plains of eastern Sabah, although clay-rich, are subject to unpredictable floods.

sometimes incorrectly lumped under the negative headings of 'shifting agriculture' or 'slash and burn'.

A 2001 study in West Kalimantan, Indonesian Borneo, of soils where swidden farming had been practised in the same area for more than 200 years, showed that concentrations of phosphorus available in the soil for uptake by plants tended to increase over the first four cycles of rice planting and fallow vegetation, and to remain stable thereafter, if the methods used were traditional, with a cycle of about 20 years between rice farming on one site. This is of significance because, throughout the humid tropics, phosphorus tends to be the element required by plants for growth and reproduction that is most limiting in soils. The Kalimantan researchers believed that the relatively high soil phosphorus concentrations in swidden farming areas were linked to the deep roots of fallow vegetation and not to fire, which tends to cause a loss of the mineral in burned topsoil.

From swidden to settled

For many decades there has been a trend in Sabah whereby communities that practised swidden farming have tended to settle as individual family units on permanent plots of a few hectares each. Such a change automatically spells the beginning of the end of their ability to be self-sufficient in food, as well as the erosion of many customs and social activities linked to rice farming. The social fabric of swidden communities that move or resettle without enough farming land will inevitably change. This trend has been ongoing, not through any particular government policy or scheme but, rather, because of several factors peculiar to Sabah.

One such factor is that Sabah's native societies have traditionally been rather egalitarian, unlike the hierarchical or feudal system that characterise some native groups in other parts of Borneo. Sabah native families tend to make decisions for themselves, rather than as a community or according to the views of a community leader. Another factor may be that the British North Borneo Company, which governed Sabah (then British

Away from the coastal lowlands, non-irrigated rice has been the staple food for Dusun and other native communities for hundreds and probably thousands of years. Hill rice is grown using a fallow system, whereby forest is allowed to regenerate after one or two planting seasons, thereby suppressing weeds that compete with rice. This 'swidden' system results in a patchwork of vegetation types over a broad landscape.

North Borneo) between 1881 and 1942, took a mercantile approach to its territory and inhabitants, favouring the growing of cash crops. This was in contrast to the Brooke family in Sarawak and the Dutch administration of Indonesian Borneo, where the general policy was to leave natives to their own devices. However, the most important factor may be that the British administration favoured granting freehold land titles to individual natives, a practice enshrined in the Land Ordinance of 1930, which has remained virtually unchanged. Possession of title to rather small individual land lots has long been an aspiration of many Sabahans, but this is incompatible with traditional swidden farming.

Orang Sungai, inhabitants of the banks of the large rivers of eastern Sabah, traditionally planted rice on the fertile riverbanks, a form of swidden farming. Scenes such as this are now rare, as most families have moved to titled plots of land near to roads, and abandoned traditional subsistence farming in favour of regular income-generating livelihoods.

The fact that Sabah's rural native communities were forced to move repeatedly even before the coming of the British, owing to aggressive neighbours or disease, demonstrates their intrinsic adaptability. One of the issues that has arisen in recent decades is that long-term settlement in defined land areas tends to mean a choice between ecologically unsustainable rice farming, or the need to seek money-generating work in order to buy rice from shops. Furthermore, in almost all rural areas young people tend to look for an alternative livelihood that does not tie them to the village for nine months of the year in food production, but instead allows them choices and the option to earn money. History elsewhere tells us that this may be an unstoppable trend.

Not by rice alone

Cultivated and wild edible fruits tend to be highly seasonal, so traditionally they are not a major source of food for people in rural Sabah. The inhabitants of many rural communities also tend to eat vegetables rarely, obtaining them only periodically by growing them scattered in rice fields, or by opportunistically harvesting the shoots of wild shrubs and ferns along riverbanks.

Instead, animal protein forms the next most important food after rice for most people in traditional rural Sabah. Although rural communities have reared livestock for many generations, this has been on a very small scale, and livestock has not traditionally been considered the main meat or protein source. Domestic pigs are kept as much to scavenge domestic waste and as sacrifices at funerals and social events as for meat, while chickens are reserved for special occasions, and buffalo are kept to plough wet rice fields. Where villages are located along larger rivers, fish are typically the first choice for protein, because they can be caught within a couple of hours after work in the rice fields, and by men or women, young or

ABOVE Bearded Pig is the favoured target of many traditional communities because in extensive forests on rather infertile soils this species tends to represent the best return on time invested in hunting. In former times, when large herds were crossing rivers, all able men would join in spearing them, and preserving the meat by smoking and drying it.

LEFT Giant freshwater prawns (*Macrobrachium rosenburgii*), found in the lower reaches of larger rivers.

old. Obtaining meat from wild mammals and birds in the forest, in contrast, takes more time, and greater effort, skills and risk.

Traditionally, wild meats are obtained by both trapping and hunting, and both activities are considered men's tasks. Generally, there would have been individuals in rural communities who particularly enjoyed hunting (or trapping), who were good at their job and who would spend much of their time thus occupied. In addition to supplying immediate family needs, hunters might give away, share, sell or barter the meat they obtained.

Of all fruits, durian (here *Durio zibethinus*) is the most prized throughout Sabah, but it is available only seasonally. A variety of mammals, such as Plantain Squirrel (*Callosciuris notatus*), compete with humans for this fruit.

For most non-Muslim communities, the favoured target of hunting is the Bearded Pig, because in extensive forests on rather infertile soils this species tends to represent the best return on time invested in hunting. In addition, many hunters operate with their trusted dogs. Finding and cornering a pig – or a Sambar Deer (*Cervus unicolor*) – is normally a task of the dogs. In former times, when there were extensive forest tracts from the lowlands up to the mountains, large herds of Bearded Pigs would build up and follow common pathways to seek and make the most of regional variations in peak times of mass fruiting. When such herds were crossing rivers within walking distance of a village, all able men would join in spearing the pigs.

Trapping tends to target a different array of species. Noose traps set on the ground usually yield mouse-deer, civets, porcupines and pheasants, while small traps set in trees around villages target squirrels and tree rats.

Other Elements of Human Life in Rural Sabah

The first monotheistic religion in Borneo was Islam, with the earliest known conversion of native people occurring around AD1408 in the Idahan community near Lahad Datu in eastern Sabah. Today, well over half of Sabah's (and Borneo's) population is Muslim, concentrated mainly in the coastal, floodplain and urban areas. The traditional religious beliefs of Sabah's main native groups, the Kadazan-Dusuns and Muruts, who live in coastal plains and inland valleys and plains, centre on a spirit world without a single deity. Now, the majority of Kadazan-Dusuns and many Muruts are Christian, a reflection of missionary work during colonial times.

In the past, health and disease had major influences on rural communities in Sabah. Smallpox and cholera epidemics account in part for the small, scattered nature of its human population prior to the mid-20th century, especially on the east-coast rivers.

Researchers trying to ascertain why there was a decline in the population of Muruts in southwestern Sabah from around 1900 to 1951, in contrast to an increase in the human population elsewhere in Sabah over the same period, concluded that the probable causes were a combination of marriage between close relatives linked to an array of debilitating diseases such as malaria. It is only in recent years that a malaria parasite common in wild macaque monkeys in Sabah, *Plasmodium knowlesi*, has been shown to infect people in rural areas. This type of malaria takes only 24 hours to complete its life cycle, which means it can achieve a high parasite density in a short time and is thus potentially fatal to humans.

Visitors to Sabah are normally safe from this malaria, although travellers in rural areas are advised to take anti-malaria prophylaxis medicine. For traditional native communities living in forested areas, however, this malaria can be more common than are colds in urban communities, and much more debilitating. The root of a small tree, Tongkat Ali (*Eurycoma longifolia*) is used traditionally in Sabah as an anti-malarial cure.

Abai, a small village at the mouth of Kinabatangan River, isolated by surrounding swamps and flood-prone land. Typically, land in rural villages is held under native titles, owned in perpetuity by natives, while surrounding forests are Forest Reserve (in the Abai case mangrove), Wildlife Sanctuary (in the Abai case Kinabatangan) or Park.

Customary law, land and forests

All societies need an agreed system of customs and rules to help ensure that, whatever social and economic system prevails, society continues to function. Most of us tend to regard laws as printed documents, the contents of which have been passed and implemented by national, regional or local governments. But unwritten customary law, often known in Borneo as *adat*, existed in all communities in Sabah before the arrival of the British. This type of law developed in the absence of formal institutions of approval, was transferred verbally and by memory down the generations, and was modified through time according to changing circumstances. Penalties for breaking *adat* – typically a fine of livestock or heirlooms – were

imposed by community leaders, and peer pressure was the main means to ensure they were enforced.

Some *adat* was put into writing, or 'codified', between 1936 and 1939 during the British North Borneo Company administration. Sabah also has Native Courts, formalised under 1992 laws, as well as subsidiary legislation on *adat*. The biggest issue regarding *adat* throughout Borneo in recent decades, however, concerns land and forest.

Clarity on who has rights over specific land and forest is of enormous significance, not only to those native communities that existed before the arrival of logging companies, plantation developers and new immigrants, but equally to the conservation of forests, wildlife and biodiversity. The British administration of North Borneo regarded forests as the domain of the government. The granting of land titles to individuals and companies was intended purely as a means to promote development, meaning the removal of forest and its replacement with something else of economic value. The Malaysian government has taken a similar view, and thus almost all forest land in Sabah is owned by the government, while almost all land that has been issued with title to individuals and companies has been converted to alternative use. In the past, land with title would most likely have been cultivated with rubber or rice, but since the 1980s oil palm has become the most popular crop. Indeed, land with title that remains under forest can in theory be taken back by the government. This state of affairs is one reason why the idea of buying land for nature conservation has not progressed far in Sabah, while such a notion may work well in other parts of the world. In recent years, however, the idea of acquiring specific land areas to act as wildlife corridors between reserves and sanctuaries has been pursued successfully, by Sabahan Cynthia Ong and others.

Competition between various interests over land in Sabah started to become intense in the 1970s, as a result of the expanding human population, expanding world markets, an explicit government policy to diversify Sabah's economy away from the logging of natural forests, and many other factors normal during the development stage of a nation.

Brunei, Indonesia and Malaysia have different concepts and laws regarding land and forest tenure. For example, under the Malaysian constitution, state-level (not federal, or district) governments have control over land and forest, while in Indonesia, governmental decentralisation has led to some ambiguity even though central government still formally retains ultimate control. Malaysia has the concept of the 'forest reserve', whereby forest and the land on which it grows are considered to be a single management entity. Although there may occasionally be disputes over small, specific sites, authority over forest reserves is simple and clear. In Indonesia, in contrast, the concept does not exist. This is a fundamental reason why forests of Indonesia remain under greater threat than those in Sabah, with many parties in Indonesian Borneo – including natives, immigrants and corporations – all competing for the same land and wood.

Sukau, another village on Kinabatangan River, originally a centre for trading of edible birds' nests and forest products, started to decline after the logging boom, which peaked here in the 1950s to 1970s. Road access (from 1984), oil palm and nature tourism gave the community a new lease of life.

In Malaysian Borneo, where 'native' is taken to mean all indigenous people and their descendants, including those who are fully urbanised, the term 'native customary rights' is used with reference to land. In Sabah, the concept of 'native' may also include assimilated immigrants who are natives of adjacent countries, as well as individuals who have only one parent or grandparent from an indigenous group. Natives form a large majority of the population – many are immigrants, many live in towns and, nowadays, most have never planted rice.

The Sabah Land Ordinance of 1930, which is still in effect, provides fairly clear and detailed definitions of 'customary rights', including occupation or cultivation of land, and land planted with fruit trees. But the definitions exclude land under natural tree cover. This means that indigenous people cannot claim customary rights over forest where they traditionally hunted and obtained forest products, and there is no automatic right of any person or community to claim ownership of fallow rice fields.

The law does, however, allow indigenous communities the option to request for the establishment of native reserves or communal land titles, which would give them control over their traditional land and allow retention of forests and fallow land. Very few such reserves have been established and no communal titles issued, largely because there was no demand from the communities. Instead, individuals have the option to secure permanent title to land – normally of up to 6ha per person. This is known as native title, which is valid in perpetuity, and may be leased, sold or used as a collateral security to obtain loans from banks. The option to obtain individual land titles has been pursued with enthusiasm from the 1930s right up to the present. Today, there is little land left that has not already been legislated as forest reserve (or park or wildlife sanctuary), or granted title to individuals or companies for development.

The road dilemma

If there is one outstanding development that has made Sabah less wild, resulted in the loss of its forests and exacerbated the risk of wild fires during El Niño droughts, it is roads. Roads – typically built by logging companies to extract wood in the 1970s and 1980s, but more recently by government as a social obligation – can bring loggers, hunters, land speculators and, potentially, social problems to previously remote communities. They are thus a two-edged sword. For the relatively few people who still live in the remotest parts of Sabah, the chances are that they have to walk for hours to get to a road, and that may be a rough, abandoned logging road. After weighing the pros and cons, most people living in such remote areas would probably like to have permanent, good road access from their farm to markets and towns. A few might not like a road, perhaps because they prefer a traditional way of life, quietness and/or other features associated with their remoteness. If the majority of people in any area want a road, and either government or business interests offer it, the best way forward therefore is to ensure that potential negative impacts are minimised, and that the benefits are long term, not temporary. It is easy to be critical of roads, but it is worth thinking about the people who have to live without them as you drive to the Danum Valley, Tabin Wildlife Reserve or Maliau Basin.

Do rural communities know best how to manage the forest?
Rural communities may be in an ideal position to manage the forests at local level, because they live nearby and because some individuals will be very familiar with the plants, animals, topography and history of their own area. Many Borneo researchers have argued for the need to work with, and secure the support of, local people in forest conservation.

Before the advent of chainsaws, rural people living in Sabah's predominantly forested landscapes struggled to keep the forest 'at bay', carving their living space and rice fields out of a natural system – the forest – that tended to regenerate wherever it had been removed. It may be that in the past Sabah's indigenous communities purposely conserved and managed the forests sustainably. However, it is more likely that, until recent times, rural communities retained extensive forests because they were small, they had no access to expensive machines, and they were less able than outsiders to pursue business opportunities.

The notion that rural communities will automatically conserve and manage local forests has never been proven. No community stays frozen in time, but will change with changing regional, national and global circumstances. The composition and individual views within rural communities change and are always changing. Neither whole communities nor individual people can suddenly move from swidden farming to full-time business or to work in service industries such as tourism.

The most active and entrepreneurial community members will tend to be those that see new opportunities, such as converting forest to plantations, or selling land.

Neither local communities nor government agencies nor NGOs have the monopoly on wisdom; sometimes it takes outsiders, including business people, to come up with a fresh and practical vision. Ultimately, every situation is different and each may require different arrangements to conserve and manage wild areas effectively. But it is no coincidence that most remaining forest in Sabah is forest reserve, that the best remaining wild forests are in protected areas, and that the regions of Sabah that are inhabited by some of the most traditional of rural communities are also areas that lost much of their forest decades ago.

The landscape of northern Sabah, although scenic, underwent extensive forest loss even before the arrival of the British, probably as a result of intensive swidden farming in the rather seasonal climate that characterises this part of the state.

The Regions

Kota Kinabalu

A tour of wild Sabah should start in Kota Kinabalu, where an important lesson can be learned: that wild and tame (or restored or fabricated) are not so much distinct opposites as two ends of a spectrum. Wherever there are patches of natural vegetation, or patches of trees that approximate in form and diversity small patches of forest, there will be some wildlife. Wildlife in urban areas does tend to consist mainly of species that are small in size and broad in ecological niche. Generally, as in most parts of the world, birds represent the most obvious wildlife in towns, attracting attention by being active in the daytime or making distinctive sounds.

One way to start a wildlife tour of the city would be to seek out a noisy flock of Asian Glossy Starlings as they congregate to roost in clumps of urban trees at dusk. Viewed by some as an invasive nuisance, this species is a native of Sabah, and has not only made towns its prime habitat, but has also been instrumental in spreading the seeds of exotic species of acacia.

OPPOSITE Map of Sabah.

BELOW Kota Kinabalu city, with Signal Hill behind the city centre, Kota Kinabalu Bird Sanctuary (regenerating mangrove) at bottom right, and the islands of Tunku Abdul Rahman Park.

In the coastal vegetation characterised by Aru, or Casuarina, trees at Tanjung Aru, along a tiny stretch of sandy coastal plain on the south side of Kota Kinabalu, can be found Blue-naped Parrots (*Tanygnathus lucionensis*), Pied Trillers (*Lalage nigra*), pigeons and sunbirds. The small tracts of mudflats on both the southern and northern fringes of the city typically attract at least one species of egret throughout most of the year. This is the habitat of the Pacific Reef Egret (*Egretta sacra*), curious in being common nowhere, even in good habitats, and in being represented by two 'phases', or colour forms, within a single species, one white and the other grey-black. A little further out to sea are found several species of tern, lighter and more graceful equivalents of the gulls that are seen on the coasts of temperate regions of the world.

From the city centre, a walk up the steps leading to the Atkinson Clock Tower – the oldest remaining building in Sabah – takes you onto the slopes of Signal Hill (also known as Bukit Bendera), where a mix of trees and strangling figs provides a habitat for pigeons, bulbuls and Plantain Squirrels (*Callosciurus notatus*). Sometimes, views can be obtained of Brahminy Kites (*Heliastur indus*), or even pairs of White-bellied Sea Eagles (*Haliaeetus leucogaster*), which live along the coastline – you may be alerted by the distant raucous, quacking calls of the latter.

At the Kota Kinabalu Bird Sanctuary, a 12ha fragment of regenerating mangrove on the inland side of Signal Hill reminds us of an era before the Second World War, when the town of Jesselton (now Kota Kinabalu city) was separated from the little coastal villages of Likas and Inanam (now northern residential fringes of the city) by sandy plains and quite extensive mangrove swamps. The sanctuary forms a refuge for a scattering of egrets, Purple Herons (*Ardea purpurea*), night herons and pigeons, apart from being the most convenient location for Kota Kinabalu residents and visitors to see close up, from a boardwalk, how mangrove ecosystems operate.

North of Kota Kinabalu, showing how the coastal highway has trapped freshwater in Likas Lagoon (left of Kota Kinabalu City Mosque), as well as creating a mixed seawater-freshwater lagoon to the right, both lagoons providing habitat for water birds. The large offshore island is Gaya.

117

White-bellied Sea Eagle (*Haliaeetus leucogaster*), one of Sabah's largest raptors, best seen from hills on the coast, such as from Signal Hill behind Kota Kinabalu.

On the inland side of the coastal highway heading northwards from the city, beyond the northern tip of Signal Hill, is Likas Lagoon, an example of how wildlife habitats can be created by human development, in this case inadvertently. The lagoon is a tract of essentially freshwater run-off from inland that became trapped by construction of the coastal highway, and is managed as a repository for excess water during heavy rainstorms. The lagoon has become very shallow at its northern end, through the settlement of sediments in the water, creating a gradation of swamp covered by sedges, grasses, shrubs and small trees to deeper open water. Likas Lagoon is now a stop-over point for migrant waders, which move to the tropics during the northern winter. Resident species that can be seen include the Little Egret (*Egretta garzetta*), Purple Heron, Striated Heron (*Butorides striata*), Cinnamon Bittern (*Ixobrychus cinnamomeus*), Wood Sandpiper (*Tringa glareola*) and White-browed Crake (*Porzana cinerea*), while migrants include the Rufous-necked Stint (*Erolia ruficollis*), Black-winged Stilt (*Himantopus himantopus*) and Grey-tailed Tattler (*Tringa brevipes*).

Islands of the South China Sea

Off the west coast of Sabah and covered by the South China Sea is a part of the Sunda Shelf, an extension of mainland Southeast Asia that includes Borneo island. The depth of the sea here is largely less than 100m – shallow in the global context – and during the Pleistocene ice ages, when sea-levels fell dramatically, the shelf was exposed as dry land. Several South China Sea islands are located within Malaysian waters, some of which can be visited on daytrips or for one or two nights from Kota Kinabalu. Attractions include diving, snorkelling, beachcombing and birdwatching – several of Sabah's bird species are confined mainly to offshore islands, including scrubfowl and imperial-pigeons.

Tunku Abdul Rahman Park

The most readily accessible islands off Sabah's west coast lie within the Tunku Abdul Rahman Park, and are all less than half an hour's boat ride from Kota Kinabalu city. The park, established in 1974, consists of five islands and their adjacent marine waters and coral reefs, and covers a total area of about 5,000ha. Part of the largest island, Pulau

Tunku Abdul Rahman Park consists of marine waters and five islands off Kota Kinabalu city, including Manukan island (top right), Sulug (top left) and Mamutik.

Gaya, is privately owned, and there are villages on the side facing Kota Kinabalu. Tropical Storm Greg swept through Pulau Gaya in the early hours of 26 December 1996, toppling most of the large trees. Pulau Sapi is an off-shoot of Gaya and, along with Pulau Manukan, is the most popular with local and foreign visitors. The quietest islands in the group are Pulau Mamutik and Pulau Sulug, both of which also have the least disturbed corals.

Pulau Tiga Park

Opposite the Klias Peninsula, a group of three islands and their adjacent marine waters, totalling 15,864ha, have been protected since 1978 as Pulau Tiga Park. Each of the islands has unique features. The park can be reached by boat from Kota Kinabalu (about 50km to the southwest) or from the small town of Kuala Penyu on the northwest coast of the Klias Peninsula (about 18km away).

Oddly, although *tiga* means 'three' in Malay, the name does not refer to the three islands, but to the three peaks of the largest of these islands, Pulau Tiga, which is about 1.5km wide by 4.5km long. The three peaks are low – less than 100m above sea-level – but they form a distinctive landmark for fishermen far away at sea. Pulau Tiga consists of land forced up by the activities of a row of mud volcanoes. A story is told that it became an island in September 1897, an event supposedly linked to an earthquake off Mindanao island, between Sabah and the southern Philippines. The last major eruption of one of the mud volcanoes occurred in 1941, and the mudflow from this event still has a distinctive tree cover, consisting mostly of Aru, or Casuarina. However, most of Pulau Tiga is forested with a variety of lowland Borneo rainforest tree species, suggesting that the island must have existed in some form since more ancient times. A network of forest trails can be followed, and the island is home to the park headquarters and offers visitor accommodation. Apart from the obvious attractions of clean, quiet beaches and opportunities for snorkelling or diving, Pulau Tiga Park usually also provides visitors the chance to see Christmas Island and Lesser frigatebirds (*Fregata andrewsi* and *F. ariel*, respectively).

The Christmas Island Frigatebird breeds only on Christmas Island, a volcanic island 1,400km northwest of Australia and 360km south of Java in Indonesia. Outside the breeding season, the birds range northwards past Sabah as far as the Andaman Islands, and then back to Christmas Island, feeding frequently and exclusively on fish and other marine life along the way. They neither swim nor walk, and obtain their food by picking up live prey from beaches or the water surface, and by snatching food from other seabirds. There are believed to be fewer than 2,000 pairs of these frigatebirds, and their numbers are declining as a result of predation of young birds by introduced ants on Christmas Island.

To the northeast of Pulau Tiga is the much smaller Pulau Kalampunian Besar, a long cay of unconsolidated coral-sand fragments. The island is almost entirely covered by sea water at high tide, and continues to change in shape with the tides and monsoon storms. Great Crested Terns (*Thalasseus bergii*) sometimes congregate at its highest end.

Pulau Kalampunian Damit (meaning Small Kalampunian Island, but often called Snake Island) is a clump of sandstone, limestone and shale blocks covered in vegetation, mostly Grand Devil's-claws Trees (*Pisonia grandis*). There are also a few wild fig trees and exotic acacias, brought in by occasional visiting fruit-eating birds. Kalampunian Damit and its surrounding waters are home to several thousands of sea snakes, notably Yellow-lipped Sea Kraits (*Laticauda colubrina*), which use the island as a safe refuge to mate and nest. Visitors most often aim to see the snakes, but this little island is home to another biological peculiarity of the Indo-Pacific oceans. The *Pisonia grandis* seeds, produced in clusters of 50–200 several times annually, exude a resin that makes them stick to feathers. Seabirds such as terns that fly past or alight on the trees act as agents of dispersal to other islands. In turn, *Pisonia grandis* must have evolved to become tolerant of the unique conditions typical of small, remote islands, where there are hardly any real soils, but instead rocks covered by guano, the accumulated phosphate-rich droppings of seabirds.

Pulau Mengalum

Partly as a result of being a veterinary quarantine site for many years, the flat 400ha Pulau Mengalum, roughly circular in shape, has remained barely inhabited even though it is just two hours' journey by fast boat from Kota Kinabalu. Today, Mengalum is best known in Sabah as the focal point of an annual international fishing tournament. It is also home to an iron anchor of uncertain origins, first officially recorded by Captain Edward Belcher in the log of HMS *Saracen* in 1854.

Tern (*Chlidonias* species), a migrant visitor to Sabah from September to April, usually seen on the coast and over coastal wetlands.

Birds that may be seen on Pulau Mengalum include the Tabon Scrubfowl (*Megapodius cumingii*), an island specialist. Small islands such as Mengalum can be viewed as a microcosm of mainland Sabah, and of the biological impacts of forest loss and fragmentation. Indeed, Mengalum received international scientific attention in 2009 when a paper was published comparing the species of butterflies, dragonflies and damselflies recorded during an expedition to the island in 1928, when it was covered in forest, with the species present in 2007, when all the original forest had been replaced by secondary growth, imported grasses and exotic weeds. It was found that six out of 14 butterfly species had disappeared from the island, while five out of the original nine dragonfly and damselfly species had been lost. These results show neatly three of the underlying themes of this book: first, that most wild species in Sabah are a part of the forest ecosystem and are prone to extinction if forest is lost; second, that many species are, however, robust to disturbance and can survive in very damaged ecosystems; and third, that retention and restoration of extensive natural forests is necessary in order to conserve the full array of original species, especially those most adapted to closed-canopy forest.

Pulau Mantanani

The Mantanani group of three islands – Pulau Mantanani Besar, Pulau Mantanani Kecil and Pulau Lungisan – is situated about 40km north of Kota Belud and is surrounded by some of the clearest water off the west coast of Sabah. Three shipwrecks are known here, the most famous being the *Eikyo Maru*, a 7,000-tonne Japanese supply ship that, on its way between Labuan and the Philippines, was torpedoed by an American submarine in October 1944. It is now covered in corals and inhabited by fish. Frigatebirds and the Mantanani Scops Owl (*Otus mantananensis*) are among the birds of interest.

Northern Sabah

Two fingers of land point northwards from northern Sabah – the Kudat Peninsula to the west and the Bengkoka Peninsula to the east – which on a map fancifully resemble the ears of an animal's head. Marudu Bay lies between the two, and to the north are several islands, the largest being Pulau Banggi and Pulau Balambangan. At the time of writing, a large new marine park is being established to encompass the waters off northern Sabah. The northernmost tip of mainland Sabah is on the Kudat Peninsula at Tanjung Simpang Mengayau. The region can be accessed by road from Kota Kinabalu, passing through the Tempasuk Plain, and from Sandakan, passing by the Bidu-bidu Hills Forest Reserve (see page 191) via Pitas and Kota Marudu.

The Regions

The two peninsulas are the only region in the state that has a seasonal annual rainfall pattern, with a peak between October and January, and a fairly pronounced dry period between February and September. From the earliest times of human settlement, this annual pattern meant that there was plenty of scope for forests in the local area to be burned by escaping fires, used by hill rice farmers throughout Borneo to clear felled vegetation prior to planting out. When the British North Borneo Company founded the town of Kudat in 1881, initially as the capital of the territory on the basis of the site's apparently strategic location, much of the northern landscape already resembled a savannah, with scattered small trees in grassland, inhabited by Sambar Deer and Tembadau.

Nowadays overshadowed by more popular nature destinations, northern Sabah was witness to some of the early impacts of human migration to the region in the late 18th century. Following volcanic eruptions on Mindanao island in the southern Philippines, settlers began to arrive in Marudu Bay and southwards down the west coast of Sabah as far as the Tempasuk Plain during the

1760s. During that period, the migrants (mainly Iranuns) played a role as slave traders for the Sulu sultanate. Their arrival gradually strengthened the power of the sultanate's outposts in northern Borneo, enabling Sulu to exert more control over what is now Sabah. By the early 19th century, the Sulu sultanate considered northern Sabah to be the most populous and profitable district in Borneo – perhaps not surprisingly, as this was the part of the great equatorial island nearest to Sulu.

At this stage, small trading settlements had developed on the lower Paitan and Sugut rivers, exporting pearls, rice and forest products, including rattan, beeswax and camphor. The latter was particularly prized by the Chinese, who are said to have preferred Paitan camphor, a major export from northern Borneo during this period. Inland natives would exchange this commodity for equivalent volumes of salt. The beeswax that was traded was obtained from the nests of wild honey bees. Today, the Kota Marudu and Kudat area is known as one of the few in Sabah where you can obtain fresh honey, with wax if desired, from bee farms run by local villagers. The people of northern Sabah are predominantly Rungus, a part of the Kadazan-Dusun ethnic group. Forest cover here remains sparse and confined to patches in a few small forest reserves, but plantations and groves of introduced acacia trees are widespread.

The Teak tree (*Tectona grandis*) is not native to Sabah, and any Teak furniture seen here is most likely to have come from factories in Java, Indonesia. There are a few Teak plantations in Sabah, the earliest of which was established near the small town of Kota Marudu (known as Bandau until 1974) by a Dutch company in 1926. Remnants of this plantation exist and are managed by the Sabah Forestry Department. Sabah has so far never been an exporter of Teak wood, although this situation may change in the future as the more recent Teak plantations grow to harvestable size.

LEFT AND OVERLEAF Coastal scenes from the Kudat Peninsula. Most of the coastline of northern Sabah consists of sandstone headlands (where waves carve strange patterns into the stone), interspersed by beaches. The trees are Aru (*Casuarina equisetifolia*).

TOP Mengaris (*Koompassia excelsa*), now rare in northern Sabah, are the favourite nesting trees of wild honey bees (*Apis* spp.). Wax from the nests, used for making high-quality candles, was a significant item of trade from northern and eastern Sabah during the heydays of the Sulu sultanate.

ABOVE Rungus people, shown here in their traditional costumes, would in days gone by have been the main harvesters of these nests.

West Coast Plains: Klias Peninsula and Tempasuk Plain

Between the foothills of the Crocker Range (see page 133) and Sabah's western coastline is a series of plains, averaging about 12–15km wide. The plains were formed largely by erosion from the Crocker Range, with clay-rich alluvium banks deposited along the rivers and their estuaries, and more extensive sandy and swampy areas between those rivers. Human colonisation of the riverbanks and other fertile areas started many hundreds of years ago, both by Kadazan-Dusun people, probably from other parts of Sabah, and by people from the kingdom of Brunei, which had already become the major regional centre of human population and trade before the arrival of Islam in Borneo. Two parts of these western coastal plains are of particular interest to the naturalist: Klias and Tempasuk.

Klias Peninsula

Sabah's second-largest river, the Padas, drains much of southwestern Sabah, via a gorge in the Crocker Range, into the South China Sea. The mouth of this massive river sees a constant passage of vast quantities of soil and rock particles, scoured by tropical rainstorms from the steep slopes of the interior mountain ranges. About 30km to the northwest lies a low hill range, parallel to the Crocker Range, between Kuala Penyu and Menumbok. Since the last ice ages, these hills have acted as a barrier, trapping the Padas River sediments and forming the Klias Peninsula.

Initially, the trapped sediments would have been barren, acidic and partly saline. Any plants growing on this inhospitable plain died but did not decay, thus initiating a process of peat accumulation. As successive generations of plants died, they built up into peat soils at rates of as much as 1cm per year. Although peat soils consist of decaying plant matter and are not very fertile, they develop above sea-level, so are not salty, and they are moist except during very long dry periods. Over time, a variety of tree species colonised the peat and developed into diverse forest. This process started probably less than 10,000 years ago and continued until very recently along much of the western and southern coasts of the island of Borneo.

The massive peat-swamp forests of Sarawak and Kalimantan have been logged commercially only during the past few decades, and a process of conversion to oil-palm plantations has only recently got underway in some areas. But the Klias Peninsula is rather different. It represents the northern tip of those massive peat swamps and, being rather near the old Brunei sultanate, its use by humans started earlier than elsewhere. From its early days, the Brunei sultanate had outlying bases along the Klias Peninsula rivers, well before the European colonisation of Borneo. The British administration built a railway along the inland fringes of the Klias peat between 1896 and 1900. These early human settlements, both Bruneian and British, initiated a process of burning the exposed layers of peat by fires that were started both deliberately and accidentally.

Mudskippers (*Periopthalamus* species) are fish that use their pectoral fins to walk on mudflats; as long as they remain wet, mudskippers can breathe through their skin and mouth. They occur throughout the intertidal zones of western and eastern Sabah.

Parts of the Klias Peninsula were probably never covered by peat but instead consist of open muddy areas, some entirely freshwater and some with saline intrusion from the sea. An example of such a site is known as Padang Teratak, an exposed muddy area enjoyed by Water Buffalo (*Bubalus bubalus*) and migrant birds, and with small, scattered populations of Proboscis Monkeys, Silver Leaf Monkeys and Long-tailed Macaques in the surrounding patches of riverine and swamp forest.

One way to see examples of the peninsula's natural habitats – including mangrove forest and Nipah Palm swamp – is to hire a small boat from the little town of Weston, from where it is possible to reach the mouth of the Padas River. Aside from waterbirds and primates, the Estuarine Crocodile is a species that may be spotted from a boat, either by the light reflected from its eyes at night, or basking on a mudflat during the daytime. As elsewhere in Sabah, the Estuarine Crocodile (which is widespread in Asia and Australasia, and can live in both saline and fresh water) was hunted to near extinction in the Klias Peninsula, although numbers have been building slowly since the 1980s. At any time of day, visitors to mudflats of the peninsula, or wherever there is at least some mangrove vegetation present, can usually also see mudskippers, small fish that live on wet mud and in very shallow saline water around the coast.

The only remaining area of peat-swamp forest in good condition on the peninsula lies within the Klias Protection Forest Reserve. Logged periodically at low intensity since the 1950s, this reserve has been a protected area since the early 1990s, and the forest appears to be regenerating towards its original plant species composition. Drainage of water from surrounding contiguous peat for agriculture, as well as fires, pose a threat to the forest, especially during long dry spells. In most areas where the forest is in good condition, two dipterocarp species, plus Jongkong (*Dactylocladus stenostachys*) and Ramin (*Gonystylus bancanus*) are dominant. Nearer to

Adult male Proboscis Monkeys (*Nasalis larvatus*) are sometimes seen swimming in the sea in coastal waters and across large rivers.

Weston, in the smaller Kampung Hindian and Nabahan forest reserves, which merge into mangroves, the original peat-swamp forest is dominated by Sempilau Laut (*Gymnostoma nobile*) and also the Melawaring, or Red Sealing-wax Palm (*Cyrtostachys renda*). Birders, meanwhile, will find the Klias peat-swamp forests a potential site to see several species that are generally confined to forests on poor soils, notably the Scarlet-breasted Flowerpecker (*Prionochilus thoracicus*), Hook-billed Bulbul (*Setornis criniger*) and Grey-breasted Babbler (*Malacopteron albogulare*).

Tempasuk Plain

The Tempasuk Plain, to the north of Kota Belud town and stretching from the Kedamaian River in the south to the Pandasan River in the north, has for long been an anomaly among Sabah's rural areas. It is the only extensive part of Sabah that seems to have lost whatever original forest cover it had, since well before the arrival of Europeans to northern Borneo. Instead, there is one great tract of about 12,000ha of open wetlands, ranging from intensively farmed rice paddies in the south, through clay-rich swamps inland, to wet, sandy marshes covered in coarse grasses and sedges on the seaward side.

OPPOSITE ABOVE Stork-billed Kingfisher (*Halcyon capensis*), a common, large kingfisher of the Klias Peninsula and large rivers and wetlands in Sabah.

OPPOSITE BELOW The Estuarine Crocodile (*Crocodylus porosus*), a widespread species of Asia and Australasia, occurs in the extensive wetlands on the south side of Klias Peninsula.

The grassy marshes support a few thousands of cattle, Water Buffaloes and small, wiry horses that have been reared by Bajau and, presumably since the 18th century, Iranun communities. The origin of the horses remains a mystery. These domesticated animals have been grazing continuously through much of the plain for hundreds of years, which has prevented tree cover from recovering by natural processes. As a result, the Temapsuk Plain has for long been a patchwork of open wetlands, serving as a major stop-off point and overwintering site for migrant birds that arrive annually from northern mainland Asia.

Ulu Padas

Ulu Padas represents the mountainous southernmost part of the Padas, Sabah's second-largest river catchment, and has an altitude extending to 2,000m above sea-level near the border with Sarawak and East Kalimantan, Indonesia. Until the early 1980s, most of the region was covered in undisturbed forests and was home to just two rather isolated groupings of human settlement.

I first visited Ulu Padas in 1981, the year of a Sabah election, and found the local Lun Dayeh and Murut inhabitants in a state of excitement because the government had promised, if returned to power, to build a road to Long Pasia, the remotest village in the region. The coolness of the climate at altitudes above 1,000m was striking, as was the fact that the ancient footpath between Sipitang and Long Pasia followed the contours of the mountainsides. Dense natural forest obscured views of more than 25m from the path, and the walking gradient rose so slowly that I could hardly imagine I was in a mountain range. Only the awareness of slopes, going up to the right and downwards to the left as I walked, showed that I really was in the mountains. This was a huge contrast to the relentless gradient climbers face when ascending or descending Mount Kinabalu.

The forests I encountered en route from Sipitang southwards were of two main sorts: either old-growth, which had never been cut, or secondary, the fallow that follows the abandonment of harvested hillside rice fields. I did not make it to Long Pasia, but instead spent time near the Murut villages of Ibul and Maligan. Red Leaf Monkeys, Bornean Gibbons and several species of hornbill were quite common away from the villages.

There were two particular highlights of my walks on this trip. One was a clear sighting of the fabulously beautiful Long-tailed Broadbill (*Psarisomus dalhousiae*); the other was a chance meeting in the forest with a young

RIGHT Bornean Gibbons and Red Leaf Monkeys (*Presbytis rubicunda*; shown here) are the primates most often encountered in the highland forests of Ulu Padas.

OPPOSITE The highland forests of Ulu Padas are characterised by trees of moderate size, mosses and frequent rain and mists.

The Regions

Murut man, out hunting Sambar Deer with his dogs in the Ketanun River valley. We were both alone and shared several insights into human beings, but I learned more from him than he from me. The first insight was that much effort is required to cut and burn forests manually, as the necessary basis for growing rice in wet climates. Borneo's indigenous people are not so much in harmony with the rainforest, but rather live with it, cutting it to grow rice and make settlements, and fishing or hunting within it for protein, which is very sparsely distributed. A more specific insight was that not everyone in a forest community is either born, or happy, or even competent to be a successful hunter. The best hunters may be considered unusual even within their own community, and happiest when hunting far from the village, either alone or with dogs. A further insight gained on that day was one that has stayed with me ever since, and has helped to guide much of my conservation work. My brief acquaintance told me that he liked to hunt in the Ketanun Valley because deer were common there. Whenever he came there, he could find Sambar Deer, in contrast to the remaining and much vaster forest areas of the Ulu Padas, where finding a deer was a rare and unpredictable event. My feeling then, and now, is that any locally high

concentrations of large mammals in rainforests are associated more with specific soils, or a juxtaposition of soil types, than with either the species composition of the local vegetation or even with the prevalence of hunting.

Following a decision by Sabah's then Chief Minister in 1981 to bring road access to the communities of Ulu Padas, and in the mid-1980s to establish a paper-making factory south of Sipitang town (still in operation), much of the upper Padas was allocated to supply wood for the new factory. The need to access these wood supplies did indeed bring roads to the Maligan and Ibul area (an old concentration of Murut tribespeople), and to the Long Pasia and Long Mio area (an old concentration of the Lun Dayeh ethnic group). The idea of cutting down tropical rainforest to

ABOVE Male Raffles's Malkoha (*Phaenicophaeus chlorophaeus*), a common resident of disturbed forests in the foothills of Ulu Padas.

LEFT Male Red Barking Deer (*Muntiacus muntjak*), along with Bearded Pigs, one of the most common large terrestrial mammals of the highland forests of Ulu Padas.

make paper was controversial, especially when the mountains are steep, and when they receive high rainfall that ultimately is the water source for many lowland communities. Aside from these environmental concerns, there is also an economic issue: building and maintaining roads in mountains to haul out wood is expensive. Following a change in ownership in 2007 of the company that makes the paper and manages the forest concession, it is intended that the focus of pulp-wood production will shift from the exploitation of natural high-mountain forests towards the expansion of industrial tree plantations concentrated in lower, more accessible areas nearer Sipitang. Extensive parts of those areas were subject to wild fires during several dry years in the 1990s, following earlier logging, so the development of new tree plantations here is expected to cause minimal biodiversity loss.

In Ulu Padas, botanists have found unusual variety in the types of forest and the plant species they contain. The flora has many similarities with mountain forests elsewhere in northern Borneo, but there are significant differences in the array of species compared to Mount Kinabalu. The local variation in forests and plant species within the Ulu Padas region is linked to local differences in soils (flat areas tend to be sandy and infertile), slope (moderate slopes tend to have the tallest trees) and altitude (the higher the land, generally the more mist and less sunshine). Some localities are rich in Borneo oaks and chestnuts of the genera *Lithocarpus*, *Quercus* and *Castanopsis*, some are dominated by native highland conifers, and some are rich in orchids and other epiphytes, several species of which were first discovered in Ulu Padas.

Crocker Range and Mount Kinabalu

Crocker Range

Named after William Crocker, Governor of North Borneo in 1887–88, the Crocker Range of forest-covered mountains forms a backbone along the western side of Sabah and rises to approximately 1,500m for most of its length.

View of the Crocker Range from the Kota Kinabalu–Tambunan road, showing the grassy peaks of Bukit Wakid (just right of centre) and the north part of the Trus Madi Range (far distance). All these mountains form important catchment areas that protect water supplies for communities below.

Seen from a distance, the Crocker mountains seem dull and bluish in colour. Geologically, they are thick layers of deformed sedimentary rocks extending to the north and northeast towards Kudat and the upper Sugut River, and encompassing Mount Kinabalu. A remarkable feature of the Crocker Mountains is the Padas Gorge, where the Padas River cuts through the range from the interior of Sabah. This represents one of the prime locations for whitewater rafting, not only in Sabah but in the whole of Southeast Asia.

Much of the Crocker Range was established as a park in 1984, although the same area was originally protected as a forest reserve in 1968 to limit cultivation and development on the steep slopes, and to protect the quality of water flowing into rivers on the west coast plains and in the interior.

Four roads cross over the Crocker Range from west to east. The northernmost of these is part of the Kota Kinabalu–Sandakan highway, which traverses the southern slopes of Mount Kinabalu and passes the entrance to Kinabalu Park. The southernmost road, which is also the newest, traverses a low pass at the narrow end of the range and skirts the northern fringes of the Sabah Forest Industries concession. The middle two roads over the range (from Penampang to Tambunan, and from Kimanis to Keningau) pass through tracts of natural highland dipterocarp and montane forest inside the Crocker Range Park. A small park headquarters is situated on the Kimanis–Keningau route, not far from Keningau town. The Penampang–Tambunan route passes through the Rafflesia Forest Reserve, where flowers of the species *Rafflesia pricei* can sometimes be seen. This road was the first motorable crossing of the Crocker Range; prior to that, residents of the eastern side of the mountains could obtain essential items such as salt only by walking over the range and down to the coast or, from in the early 20th century, by taking a train from Tenom via the Padas Gorge. Serious trekkers can still walk over the Tambunan–Penampang part of the Crocker Range on trips lasting three days or more, following a route often called the 'salt trail'.

Mahua waterfall, on the east side of the Crocker Range north of Tambunan town, is accessible by four-wheel-drive vehicle, and represents one of numerous small rivers that cascade down the mountain range to provide clean water to villages and farms in the foothills and plains below.

LEFT Blue-winged Pitta (*Pitta moluccensis*), a migrant that may be seen on islands and coastal lowlands, and on the highest parts of the Crocker Range from October to April.

BELOW LEFT Banded Pitta (*Pitta guajana*), a ground-dwelling resident of mountain forests.

Alternative ways to see the lower parts of the Crocker Range, including its lowland and hill dipterocarp forest, are to visit the fringes south of Kota Kinabalu, at the Inobong substation of the Crocker Range Park, or Sugud Recreation Forest or Kampung Kituau. Birdwatchers looking for lowland forest species find that these sites offer an alternative to the east side of Sabah.

On fine days, outstanding aerial views of the Crocker Range can be obtained from daily scheduled aeroplane services that depart from either Lahad Datu or Tawau to Kota Kinabalu. These flights pass quite low over the middle part of the range en route to the state capital.

Mount Kinabalu

With its highest peak reaching 4,095m above sea-level, Mount Kinabalu is the tallest mountain between Myanmar (Burma) and Papua in Indonesian New Guinea. The top is bare granite, while the lower slopes are covered in farms and settlements. In between is a variety of natural tropical rainforests, their individual differences linked to local differences in soil, temperature, light and exposure to wind. Mount Kinabalu occupies the southern end of a much bigger (766sq km) tropical rainforest protected area, Kinabalu Park.

After Mount Kinabalu's imposing physical presence – and the fact that it is often wet, misty, windy and cold – the most prominent feature of the mountain is its diverse flora. Many eminent botanists have tried to create a simple classification of Mount Kinabalu's vegetation zones for the layman, but in practice this has never really been possible, in large part because of the sheer large numbers of species within various plant groups, from tiny herbs, ferns and mosses, to shrubs, orchids and other epiphytes, to trees. In turn, the diversity of plants and the vegetation structure, along with shifts in climate and vegetation zonation up and down the mountain during the Pleistocene ice ages, have resulted in a diversity of animal life.

Its close proximity to Kota Kinabalu has made Mount Kinabalu a globally unique magnet for naturalists. The headquarters of Kinabalu Park itself is reached within just two hours from the state capital, and is set on the park's southern boundary at an altitude of 1,564m in a zone of lower montane forest. In the middle of the park lies Mount Tambuyukon (2,579m), the third-highest mountain in Borneo. It comprises ultrabasic rock, and is visited only very rarely, even by keen botanists and mountaineers. Further north still are extensive forested hill ranges encompassing the upper fringes of dipterocarp forest, the tall forests that were once Borneo's most extensive natural vegetation type.

One of the botanical pioneers of Mount Kinabalu, Lilian Gibbs of the British Museum, visited the mountain in February 1910, setting off south by train from Jesselton (now Kota Kinabalu) through the Padas Gorge to Tenom, then travelling by horse to Tambunan and, finally,

northwards on foot. In addition to collecting over 1,000 plant specimens and being the first woman to ascend to Kinabalu peak, she made a basic classification of the vegetation types. In 1914, Miss Gibbs listed 203 plant species from Mount Kinabalu, but by the time American John Beaman published his research in 1989, the list had reached almost 4,000 from the same general area. The Sabah Parks authorities suggest that perhaps an additional 2,000 plant species exist in the other mountains and hills within the park.

Sabah's flagship natural feature, Mount Kinabalu (4,095m), has a top of bare granite, and a variety of vegetation types stretching down to the cultivated foothills.

On the lower slopes of Mount Kinabalu up to around 1,000m, most of the original vegetation has been cleared, either to grow hill rice on a fallow system, or to plant crops such as rubber and vegetables. Much of what appears to be forest in this lower zone is, in fact, secondary growth of fast-growing trees, some of which are native and some introductions such as Para Rubber (*Hevea brasiliensis*) and acacias. However, to the east and north of Mount Kinabalu, and most accessible at Poring (see below), there are tracts of original hill dipterocarp forest up to and beyond this altitudinal zone.

From 1,000m to 1,800m (the zone in which Kinabalu Park headquarters sits) is lower montane forest rich in Bornean species of oaks, laurels, myrtles and conifers. These plant families are typically associated with northern hemisphere temperate and Mediterranean climates, but their species diversity is highest in the hills and mountains of Borneo. Between 1,800m and 3,200m is mossy forest of lower stature, where mosses drape tree trunks and branches. Between the sedimentary rocks of the lower slopes and the granite peak above is a narrow intervening layer of ultrabasic rock, at around 2,750–3,000m, with its own type of scrub forest. Above 3,000m is the granite dome of Mount Kinabalu, with dwarf scrub forest, while above 3,700m cold winds and rain frequently lash the mountaintop, which is almost devoid of plant life.

The first person known to have reached the highest point of Kinabalu (Low's Peak, which is ascended daily by climbers now) was the ornithologist John Whitehead (the unfortunate earlier pioneers Hugh Low and Spenser St John inadvertently reached a slightly lower peak in 1858).

OPPOSITE PAGE
TOP LEFT Indigo Flycatcher (*Eumyias indigo*), the commonest flycatcher in montane forests.

TOP RIGHT Sunda Laughingthrush (*Garrulax palliatus*), a species of the lower canopy in lower montane forests.

BOTTOM LEFT Flowers of the orchid *Renanthera bella*.

BOTTOM RIGHT The slipper orchid *Paphiopedilum rothschildianum*, one of Kinabalu's most famous plants. Both orchids are confined to ultrabasic soils at lower elevations.

From January to April 1887, in an era when the collection of wildlife specimens was not only acceptable but indeed necessary in order to be able to describe and name 'new' species, Whitehead obtained 300 bird specimens from Mount Kinabalu, 18 of them new to science. During an even more gruelling return visit between January and May 1888, Whitehead reached Low's Peak on 11 February, with four local Dusuns and two Kadayans. These two scientific expeditions, during which Whitehead collected not only birds but also other vertebrates and invertebrates, were regarded by his scientific contemporaries in Europe as among the most successful of the era. Three of Borneo's most colourful bird species – Whitehead's Broadbill (*Calyptomena whiteheadi*), Whitehead's Trogon (*Harpactes whiteheadi*) and Whitehead's Spiderhunter (*Arachnothera juliae*) – were discovered by the ornithologist on Mount Kinabalu and named after him by museum colleagues. All three bird species were subsequently found to occur on other high mountains of northwestern Borneo.

More than 300 bird species are now known from the Mount Kinabalu area, of which about 40 are seasonal migrants and 23 are endemic to Borneo. Visitors to the Kinabalu Park headquarters can expect to see noisy groups of Chestnut-capped Laughingthrushes (*Garrulax mitratus*), diminutive Black-capped White-eyes (*Zosterops atricapillus*), solitary, raucous Bornean Treepies (*Dendrocitta cinerascens*), Mountain Tailorbirds (*Orthotomus cuculatus*) and Scarlet Sunbirds (*Aethopyga mystacalis*). At higher altitudes along the main trail, from 2,500m to the uppermost vegetation, are found Mountain Blackeyes (*Chlorocharis emilae*), Kinabalu Friendly Bush-warblers (*Bradypterus accentor*) and Borneo Island Thrushes (*Turdus poliocephalus seebohmi*).

On the eastern edge of Kinabalu Park is an area known as Poring, the name referring to the giant-stemmed *Gigantochloa levis* bamboo that is locally common here. Poring is best known for its natural sulphurous hot-water spring, channelled into baths that provide climbers welcome relief after an ascent of Mount Kinabalu. Nowadays, the area has great scarcity value in supporting one of the most readily accessible natural dipterocarp forests on the western side of Sabah. Birdlife is different here from that found at higher elevations on Mount Kinabalu. An aerial walkway in the Poring forest allows views from within and above the tree canopy. Two species of *Rafflesia* also occur in the region.

Another way to see the vegetation and traditional land use of the lower slopes of Mount Kinabalu is to visit the village of Kiau, accessible by rough road off the highway from Kota Kinabalu to Kinabalu Park. This site has historical interest, as it was the last inhabited stop for early climbers of the mountain prior to the Second World War, and the place at that time to seek the most experienced guides and porters.

My first visit to Kinabalu Park, with a team of Sabah Parks rangers, was in 1979, to conduct a reconnaissance survey of the Mount Madalon peak in its far north. One of the team members was Alim Biun, one of Sabah's most knowledgeable naturalists. I first climbed Mount Kinabalu in 1980 with four companions, staying overnight at Panar Laban. We took our own sleeping bags, stove, kerosene, potatoes and vegetables, and had not imagined that we would feel so cold that we could not sleep. That memory allows me to appreciate the facilities that are available to today's climbers. The first annual Mount Kinabalu International Climbathon mountain race was held in 1987, amid grumbles from some quarters that this event would attract too much attention and too many climbers to the mountain, more litter and erosion of the trail, and a type of tourist with a less refined appreciation of nature. Now, however, we can see from the story of Mount Kinabalu and people climbing it that the concept of 'carrying capacity' in nature tourism is rather subjective, and that with good management practices nature is more robust that we might imagine.

Interior Sabah: Tambunan to Tenom

Tambunan is the name of both a small town and a unique, broad valley landscape, 600–700m above sea-level, dominated by wet rice fields, some carved as terraces on the eastern foothills of the Crocker Range. Above the rice fields, on the lower slopes of the Crocker Range and, to the east, the Trus Madi mountain range, are great groves of bamboo interspersed with rubber gardens. Stream water here is clean, as it comes from the two mountain ranges on either side of the valley. A unique culture has developed here, self-sufficient in rice, some of which is turned into wine, and making use of the bamboo for fencing, roofing and construction of small houses in the rice fields, and as pipes for channelling water from forest streams.

Trus Madi peak (2,649m), to the southeast of Tambunan town, is an outlier of the Crocker Range and the second-highest mountain in Borneo. Great swathes of its forests were selectively logged during the timber boom years of the 1980s and early 1990s, one of the attractions being large *Agathis* trees, a relative of the kauris of Australasia, then locally common on the upper ridges. The logging roads, now abandoned, made this previously remote area readily accessible for a decade. The forests have since been allowed to regenerate, and it is anticipated that in the future this mountain will become an alternative destination to Kinabalu for naturalists.

A third Sabah species of *Rafflesia* was discovered on the lower southeastern slopes of Trus Madi in the mid-1980s. This species differs from the others in being a uniform warm orange colour, resembling the glowing embers of a fire, and was named *Rafflesia tengku-adlinii* in honour of the great Malaysian conservationist and adventurer Tengku D.Z. Adlin. Shortly after its discovery, the species was found again in the centre of the Maliau Basin. Bizarrely, however, it has never been found anywhere else other than these two sites, and so is clearly a very rare species.

Rafflesia keithii, one of Sabah's three species of this parasitic plant, which may be seen in the forest at Poring and in Tenom Agricultural Park.

Driving southwards from Tambunan to Keningau, the landscape changes gradually from fertile rice fields, through a jumble of steep valleys. At Keningau is another, different sort of inland plain, one that is characterised more by pale-coloured sandy soils and deposits of gravel, pebbles and boulders that have tumbled down from the Crocker Range over geological timescales. The Kimanis–Keningau road was built over the Crocker Range in the mid-1970s (see above), to transport logs from the interior of Sabah down to the west coast. As with all timber booms anywhere in the world, logs were felled and trucked out almost continuously, in this case over a period of two decades. Wood-processing factories were established around the Keningau Plain in the 1980s and 1990s, in part a result of a ban on the export of round logs. Today, there are hardly any wild timber trees left in the Keningau region and the factories are abandoned, but the rapid expansion in the human population that accompanied the timber boom years is still evident. Oil palm has been planted extensively in this region following the demise of the timber industry, but although there are extensive, relatively flat areas, the soils and climate are not as ideal for this crop as in the eastern lowlands.

Tenom, which like Tambunan refers to both a small town and an agricultural region, sits at 300m above sea-level and was the first part of Sabah's interior to be opened up and developed with rubber and other crops. The main stimulus was the arrival of the railway, built along the Padas Gorge in the early 1900s. Tenom also has fertile soils, and a climate characterised by moderate rainfall throughout the year and temperatures lower than on the west coast plains. Tenom Agricultural Park is hardly wild, but it offers a convenient way to see a remarkable variety of native and exotic tropical plants in one place. Here, hundreds of tropical crop species, fruit trees, orchids and ornamentals can be seen within the space of a few hours. The park is an extension of a remarkable governmental agricultural research station, which focused on crop diversification rather than on just one or a few conventional species. Both the original research station and the park were developed between the mid-1970s and 1990s by senior agricultural officer Tony Lamb, who has a special interest in orchids and other native plants that may have horticultural prospects. The park also offers a chance for those who want to see a *Rafflesia* flower but find none in bloom in the Crocker Range or near Poring. The species at Tenom is *Rafflesia keithii*, and is special in representing the successful outcome of a project to inoculate the host vine, *Tetrastigma*, with *Rafflesia* seeds obtained from Poring. The Tenom Park managers waited nearly 10 years between inoculation and first flowering in 2004.

The South-east: Maliau Basin and Tawau Hills

Maliau Basin

The Maliau Basin is unique Borneo in that it is home to some of the island's most spectacular geological features. It is also important in that it is still wild – because the area has had few human visitors either in the past or now, the entire natural vegetation cover is probably ancient and undisturbed. Despite this, it is relatively accessible, and can be reached by road within a day from Kota Kinabalu via Keningau and Sapulut, or from Tawau. There are, however, no roads inside the basin itself, only designated walking trails and established campsites.

Golden-naped Barbet (*Megalaima pulcherrima*) is one of nine barbet species in Sabah. It is found in mountain ranges and in Maliau Basin.

The basin is a giant saucer-shaped depression at an altitude of 300–1,600m, enclosed by a mountainous rim about 25km across, and is covered in a variety of natural forest types. Its special features include the Maliau Falls (a series of seven waterfalls), a gorge, the north rim escarpment and Lake Linumunsut (actually outside the basin, and accessible only from the north). The Maliau Basin was provisionally designated in 1982 as a conservation area within the Sabah Foundation logging concession, and in 1997 became a formal protection forest reserve.

Entering the Maliau Basin by road from the south, visitors have a chance to spot Tembadau and a wild banana species endemic to Borneo, *Musa borneensis*. At Agathis Camp (outside the basin, and the nearest camp to the main road), an unusual combination of typical lowland and hill dipterocarp forest can be seen, together with Mengilan (*Agathis borneensis*), a large coniferous tree more commonly associated with higher elevations. During a day's walk from Agathis Camp, visitors can ascend the southern, low rim of the basin through dipterocarp and lower montane forests into a large tract of unusual upland heath forest above 900m elevation. The main Belian Camp is located outside the basin, on its southeast side, near the confluence of the Maliau and Kuamut rivers.

At a very general level, three main soil types can be distinguished within and around the Maliau Basin, each with its own associated vegetation: yellow clay soils, rich in dipterocarps and palms; white sand soils, which bear low, dense heath forest; and yellow sandy soils, which support few dipterocarps or palms but more oaks, myrtles and conifers. During dry spells, the Maliau River is a clear dark reddish colour, a characteristic arising from the presence of humic acids, produced by, and washed from, the very slowly decaying leaf litter beneath the heath forests and highest montane forests. After heavy rain, the river may rise in depth by more than 2m, when the water becomes a dense chocolate colour due to rapid natural erosion of soil particles from the prevailing steep slopes.

Maliau Falls, one of the features of Maliau Basin, which can be reached from Agathis camp (which has an access road) via a two-day walk. The lowest of the seven waterfalls has a drop of 28m.

Being at a predominantly high altitude, with rugged terrain and rather poor soils, the Maliau Basin is not a prime area for large mammals. Rather, its significance for fauna lies in the great diversity of smaller animals it supports, and in the variety of undisturbed wild forests. Birdlife here includes the Bulwer's Pheasant (*Lophura bulweri*), all eight of Sabah's hornbill species, all nine Bornean barbet species, and more than 20 endemic Bornean species from a variety of families.

In 1988, I joined an expedition to the Maliau Basin, arranged by the Sabah Foundation and WWF-Malaysia, during which a large group of researchers was flown into its centre by Royal Malaysian Air Force helicopter. One memory from that time includes the finding, by veteran Sabah biologist Joseph Gasis, of a shard of celadon ceramic, as he poked at random into the soil with his jungle knife during a breather on a hike on the last day of the expedition on the slopes south of Rafflesia Camp. This site must be one of the remotest in Sabah, yet evidently someone had passed by, probably more than a century before, and for some reason left part of a broken pot there. Another memory is of observing a group of six or so of one of the world's weirdest squirrels, unique to Borneo, known as the Red-bellied Sculptor Squirrel (*Glyphotes simus*). This little squirrel has two lower incisor teeth that have a concave front surface and splay outwards in a V shape. I watched them at eye-level, across a narrow, deep valley, as they hung upside down from the outermost twigs of a large strangling fig, high above the ground, running their odd little teeth along the central vein on the underside of the fig leaves. Whether this action was to scoop tiny insects into their mouth, or perhaps to scrape off and eat a fungus growing on the leaf, remains one of the numerous unstudied biological mysteries of wild Sabah's rainforest ecosystems.

Tawau Hills

For birders and botanists, Tawau Hills Park is possibly Sabah's best-kept secret, yet its entrance lies within an hour's drive of Tawau town. Within the park is a spectrum of undisturbed lowland dipterocarp forest, rising through hill and highland dipterocarp forest to the 1,310m peak of Magdalena.

Shorea faguetiana, one of five dipterocarp tree species measured in Tawau Hills to exceed 80m in height.

The park was established initially and primarily as a water catchment for rivers flowing to Tawau and other small settlements in the region. Its geology is unusual, in that it is largely volcanically derived. Although only 28,000ha in extent, the park adjoins more than 50,000ha of regenerating logged dipterocarp forest in adjacent protection forest reserves, effectively forming a much larger conservation area. Like the Danum Valley (see page 154), the Tawau Hills are home to a rare and localised form of the Red Leaf Monkey, which is cream-coloured but not albino.

The lowlands below and to the south and east of the Tawau Hills were among the first natural forest areas in Sabah to be converted to commercial plantation agriculture, dating back to before the Second World War and initially involving mainly Japanese interests. Further conversion of forest occurred from the 1950s onwards, with

TOP Male Olive-backed Sunbird (*Nectarinia jugularis*), a common bird of lowland forest edges that feeds on insects and nectar.

LEFT The pale form of the Red Leaf Monkey (*Presbytis rubicunda*), which occurs in Tawau Hills and in forests northwards to Danum Valley.

OPPOSITE Male Blue-headed Pitta (*Pitta baudii*), a Borneo endemic found in Tawau Hills and Danum Valley.

cocoa the favoured crop because both the local climate and soils were found to be ideal. Some people involved in those early plantation developments recall that many of the trees on the deep, rich volcanic soils were of massive stature. More recently, those subjective memories received tangible support, when in 2007 Roman Dial brought to global attention the world's tallest tropical rainforest tree, found in the Tawau Hills. This *Shorea faguetiana* (a species known locally as Seraya Kuning Siput) measured 88.3m tall. In the same area, five other dipterocarp species more than 80m tall were measured. Possibly, there are a few slightly taller individual trees elsewhere at other sites. It now seems likely, however, that before the era of the chainsaw and bulldozer, volcanic soils on low ridges supported the tallest individual trees and most dense stands of dipterocarps the world has ever seen. Old foresters used to say that the really massive dipterocarp forests were in parts of eastern Sabah and on the larger islands of the southern Philippines, where the soils are also of volcanic origin. All those forests have now gone – except on the southern fringes of Tawau Hills Park.

My first visit to Tawau Hills was with Sabah Parks rangers in 1980, soon after the establishment of the park. It was here that I learned that the absence of a particular species in a given area may be as significant as its presence. From talking to local people, including Ibans who had come to the area from Sarawak in the 1950s, it was clear that, despite the magnificent nature of the forest and the fact that most of the Tawau region had been totally uninhabited until the early 20th century, the area was devoid of Bornean Orang-utans except for occasional old males wandering in from the north and west. Even in the presence of forest rich in wild 'fruit trees' and the absence of hunting, orang-utans do not normally form breeding populations in areas that are not at low altitude, and that lack a variety of soil types.

After looking at the forest in the park, we spent six days in the surrounding plantations, which at that time were mainly old cocoa groves. Over this period, we saw more than 20 bird species within the areas planted with cocoa. At the same time, my colleague Glyn Davies investigated wildlife in Sabah Softwoods plantations of four exotic tree species to the west of Tawau Hills. Our brief observations indicated some conclusions that have since become more formally apparent from subsequent detailed studies. One is that plantations can support some wildlife species, but only a small 'subset' of the original array of species that would have been present in the natural forest. In addition, this subset is of species that are quite common and widespread in a variety of disturbed habitats. Second, natural forest forms a refuge for many of the species that may be encountered in plantations. Thus, while a few birds and mammals may live, feed and even breed within plantations, there are also species that need forest for nesting or for food when there is none in the plantation. Third (and this is especially true for birds), the structure of a habitat is of some significance, as much as the exact species composition of the plants. Old cocoa plantation, for example, mimics natural secondary forest. Fourth, it was concluded that some leguminous trees (of the bean family) provide a disproportionately high amount of biological production that may be eaten by animals, both invertebrate and vertebrate. For example, the *Albizia falcataria* wood plantations in 1980 were full of birds and some mammals, largely as a result of a massive production of tender young leaves, which were eaten by insects upon which the birds fed.

Semporna and its Offshore Islands

Situated on the Sabah mainland near Semporna town is Bukit Tengkorak, which means 'Skull Hill'. The hill is a remnant of one of many volcanic crater rims that dot the local landscape. People were making clay pots at Bukit Tengkorak several thousand years ago, bringing wet clay up from the base of the hill to its top, most likely choosing this site to catch and funnel sea breezes through boulders to fire the clay. Most remarkably, however, flecks of a naturally formed glass, called obsidian, found at Bukit Tengkorak have been shown to most likely originate from the island of New Britain, 3,500km away at the eastern end of the island of New Guinea. Dating of charcoal at the site suggests that the obsidian has been at Bukit Tengkorak for at least 3,000 years. The origin and fate of the people who lived around the hill, apparently for a period of about 2,000 years, is unknown. Further inland on the Semporna Peninsula, surrounded by plantations, is Mount Pock Forest Reserve, a fine remnant of the magnificent forest that once covered this region.

Semporna is best known for its offshore islands, some of which (Sibuan, Maiga, Mantabuan, Selakan, Bodgaya and Boheydulang) are incorporated into the Tun Sakaran Marine Park. The islands have an array of origins, with the last three being an extension of an old volcanic chain stretching between Tawau Hills and Sulu in the southern Philippines. The spectacular Pulau Bodgaya and Pulau Boheydulang are the remnants of the rim of a massive extinct volcano, while the surrounding islands are clumps and cays of coral sand. The larger islands support several rare wild plant species that have affinities to the natural flora of the Philippines rather than Borneo. Two of these, *Dracaena multiflora* and the Milk Bush (*Euphorbia lacei*), as well as the biologically ancient Cycad (*Cycas rumphii*), all of which grow as scrub thickets on the hilltops, look like plants from a desert rather than a rainforest region. A 1998 botanical expedition found at least eight plant species not known from elsewhere in Borneo.

The essence of the Semporna islands: clear shallow sea, stilt houses, shifting coral sands, sea grass, and a variety of marine animal life such as *Tridacna* clam shells and seastars (Class Asteroidea). As these habitats become depleted by decades of over-exploitation and pollutants, the establishment and sustained management of marine protected areas with limited human use represents probably the only way to ensure that they do not eventually disappear entirely.

Semporna and its islands provide the most obvious remaining historical link between the coast of northeast Borneo and the old Sulu sultanate, which had its base on Jolo Island in the southern Philippines. The chain of islands between Semporna and the southern Philippines is inhabited largely by Bajau and Suluk (also known as Tausug) people, many of whom continue their traditional way of life. In particular, the Sea Bajau depend largely on harvesting marine life for sale and barter.

For years, Semporna has been the gateway for visitors to Malaysia's sole oceanic island, Pulau Sipadan, iconic for its steep drop-off and fabulous diving. Today, there is an increasing array of opportunities for diving, snorkelling and other marine activities from the various islands off Semporna, eastwards towards the border with the Philippines and southwards towards the border with Indonesia. This area represents the western fringes of the Coral Triangle region, which extends to the western Pacific and contains globally significant coral reefs and marine biodiversity.

BELOW Semporna, the name of a district, town (shown here) and offshore zone, which represents the western fringes of the Coral Triangle.

OPPOSITE ABOVE Green Turtle (*Chelonia mydas*) in the sea off Semporna (male mating, the female is beneath the sea surface).

OPPOSITE BELOW Houses of Sea Bajau people.

OVERLEAF
LEFT Groves of old coconut palms form a distinctive backdrop to seaside villages on the Semporna islands.

RIGHT A closer glimpse of a Nipah thatch house.

Lahad Datu: Ulu Segama Malua, Danum Valley and Tabin

Ulu Segama Malua and the Danum Valley can be reached within two to three hours by road from Lahad Datu town. Visitors can expect to see a diversity of lowland bird species here, and will have a fair chance of spotting wild Bornean Orang-utans or Borneo Elephants, as well as a variety of smaller mammals, especially in the primary forest around the Borneo Rainforest Lodge and at the Danum Valley Field Centre. A drive along the road through the logged forests at night-time provides the opportunity of seeing civets, deer, flying squirrels and other nocturnal mammals.

The Tabin Wildlife Reserve is on the Dent Peninsula, an hour and a half by road from Lahad Datu town.

Ulu Segama Malua

To the west of Lahad Datu town lies a large tract of lowland and hill forest that encompasses the upper part of the Segama River catchment and the southern catchment of the Kinabatangan River. Historically, this region contained very sparse human occupation. With the conversion of most of eastern Sabah's extreme lowland forests to plantations over the past few decades, the regenerating logged forests of Ulu Segama Malua (about 240,000ha) and the old-growth forests of the Danum Valley Conservation Area (about 43,000ha) now represent the single most important habitat in Malaysia for the Bornean

Borneo Elephants bathe in the Bole River, Ulu Segama Forest Reserve.

Orang-utan and Borneo Elephant, as well as for a great variety of other wildlife, including the Red Leaf Monkey and the rare and rarely seen Bay Cat, endemic to Borneo.

Most of this region underwent intensive commercial logging from the 1960s up to 2007, when the government of Sabah fulfilled a commitment to halt the industry and allow a long fallow period for restoration of the natural forest cover. Ulu Segama and Malua are both still commercial forest reserves, gazetted as such for conservation and restoration purposes. Their names refer to the major rivers that lie within their areas: the Ulu Segama flows into the lower Segama River, while the Malua River flows northwards into the Kinabatangan River.

Parts of Ulu Segama have been very much degraded by a combination of logging and fire in 1983, which wiped out much of the original tree cover as well as some

The northern fringes of Ulu Segama have been degraded by a combination of logging and fire, which, during an El Niño drought in 1983, wiped out much of the original tree cover. A programme to restore these burned areas to a functioning forest ecosystem commenced in 2008, with the main aim of improving habitat quality for rare wildlife, especially the Bornean Orang-utan.

entire tree species locally. A major conservation programme in these areas commenced in 2008, with the aim of restoring a functioning dipterocarp forest ecosystem and the quality of habitat for rare wildlife, especially the Bornean Orang-utan. Funds for the work are sourced from the government of Sabah, several Malaysian and overseas corporations and foundations, and NGOs such as WWF-Malaysia.

Danum Valley

One large tract of forest in the Ulu Segama region was left untouched during the first round of logging in the late 1970s to 1980s, and was far enough from centres of human activities during the El Niño droughts of the late 20th century to escape the ravages of fire. That area – the Danum Valley Conservation Area – is now is one of the jewels in Sabah's crown of rainforest conservation, with not only biological but also geological, historical and scientific research interest. The field studies centre on the eastern edge of the valley is judged one of the finest tropical forest research sites in the world.

The origins of the Danum Valley as a conservation area seem to go back a long way. In 1961, Peter Burgess of the North Borneo Forest Department wrote: 'A proposal was made in 1933 to reserve a considerable area in the upper Segama and Tingkayu drainages (the latter being immediately south of Ulu Segama) in order to protect the rhinoceros, but this proposal had to be abandoned due to opposition by timber interests.' The proposal was revived in 1970, when, according to geologist K.M. Leong, officers of the Forest Department recommended that Ulu Segama be gazetted as a game reserve. Mr Leong himself explored the Danum Valley in 1968. Surveys carried out for a state-wide land capability classification report in the early 1970s noted the presence of 'game' (large mammal species preferred by hunters) along the Danum River. At that period, there would undoubtedly have been even more 'game' in the extensive flat lowlands of the lower Segama and Kinabatangan rivers. But, as with many conservation success stories, luck and timing played bigger roles than science or planning.

Danum Valley at night, when the only sounds are of chirping insects, honking frogs, and the occasional calls of owls or distant male orang-utans or elephants. This is the time to look for civets, wild cats, gliding mammals and nocturnal primates.

ABOVE LEFT Male Diard's Trogon (*Harpactes diardii*), a lowland forest bird found at Danum Valley and other tall lowland forests.

ABOVE RIGHT Male Banded Kingfisher (*Lacedo pulchella*), an uncommon bird of tall forests.

The director of the newly established WWF-Malaysia, Ken Scriven, visited Sabah in 1973, meeting with state government officials. This set in motion a scientific expedition in 1976 to the Danum Valley, with the Royal Malaysian Air Force ferrying in participants. Although some expedition participants had reservations over the suitability of the valley as an ideal conservation area, owing to its prevailing steepness and remoteness, the final report summarised the area's very high level of biological richness (biodiversity being a term yet to be invented) and endorsed the idea that it should become a national park. The final version of the land capability classification report, published in 1976, made a similar recommendation. But then the plan ran into a problem. Danum Valley, as a part of the upper Segama River catchment, was inside a logging concession granted initially to the Weyerhauser group of USA and, subsequently, for 100 years, to the Sabah Foundation. A 1981 report on a faunal survey of Sabah, carried out jointly by the Sabah Forest Department and WWF-Malaysia, endorsed the recommendation for a Danum Valley conservation area. As with the Maliau Basin (see page 141), the idea of protecting the Danum Valley intact was taken up in 1982 by Dr Clive Marsh, when he joined the newly established wildlife conservation division of the Sabah Foundation.

My first attempt to visit the Danum Valley was in April 1983, by boat, with local Dusun Segama men and Dr Marsh, along with Indian herpetologist Dr Romulus Whitaker, who was undertaking a survey of the distribution of crocodiles in Sabah. By luck, the timing happened to be just as the peak effects of the 1982–83 El Niño drought were taking hold in Sabah, and essentially becoming out of control. Much of the riverbank vegetation from the Segama ferry (now a bridge, at Bukit Belacon) up to the mouth of the Bole River was on fire or smouldering. The Segama River level was lower than it had been for decades, and we struggled to get the boats over sandbanks and exposed gravel and boulder beds. At the mouth of the Bole Besar River, where we abandoned our journey, we saw the remains of a gold-dredging machine, normally submerged, that had been dragged up the river in 1900 but abandoned after it was found that gold quantities in the riverside sediments were minuscule.

My second attempt to reach Danum was later in 1983, again with Dr Marsh and Yuya Paloh. In 1981, Yuya, a nightwatchman at the Sepilok Orang-utan Rehabilitation Centre, had saved me from an irritable bear that had escaped from its cage and broken into my house; he later passed away in the forest at Malua. This time we set off from Silam and walked westwards from the end of the logging road, which at that time was around the current junction between the Danum Valley Field Centre and Borneo Rainforest Lodge. Little did we know that this would be, for all of us, one of our worst rainforest experiences. We trekked along the trace of a proposed new logging road in primary forest, which followed the contour of the land, some tens of metres below the ridge tops. This trip taught me that, far from following proposed road traces, or even rivers, the best way to travel long distance in primary Borneo rainforest where there are no existing human trails is to stick to the ridge tops wherever possible. Whatever one may hope or plan from pondering over a topographical map, ridge tops almost always turn out to be straighter, shorter and less ambiguous than any alternative landform for long-distance walking.

On the day we walked westwards towards Danum, we slipped and slithered on moist soil, as the planned road trace followed a seemingly endless looping course along the slope below the ridge. Occasionally we fell onto the tips of saplings, whose stems had been cut off at a 60-degree angle with sharp parangs by the road surveyors. A team of three is just nice for many forms of forest expedition, as they stick together better than a larger group and can more readily make one compact yet sufficient camp. In this case, however, the terrain and our packs had slowed us down to a snail's pace by late afternoon, and we arrived after nightfall at the bank of the Segama River near its confluence with the Sapat Kalisun tributary. The banks of the rivers were steep, muddy, unstable and covered in thick shrubs. Exhausted, and seeing plenty of stars but no clouds, we decided simply to lay down on a gravel bank in the Segama River and sleep in the open. Some people fall into a deep slumber when very tired, but I was unable to sleep, my body depleted of water and salt after a long, sweaty day. At one o'clock in the morning, I became aware of a terrific distant roaring that I could not place, but that was too constant to be thunder or an animal. I then realised that, sometime soon, it was likely that we would be inundated

by a flash flood. We scrambled up the banks into thickets of wild gingers and spiny shrubs. True enough, a broad brown wall of water, carrying with it bobbing branches and other debris, soon inundated our gravel bank, and we crouched in the thicket with ants and mosquitoes until morning.

Research and conservation progammes

The Ulu Segama Malua and Danum Valley areas are home to several pioneering programmes of scientific and conservation interest. Most prominent is the Danum Valley Field Centre, opened in 1986, which is the base for many scientific studies relating to tropical rainforest ecology,

The forests of the Ulu Segama and Danum Valley area represent accessible examples of old growth and logged lowland dipterocarp forests, which have been the subject of various pioneering programmes of scientific and conservation interest. Danum Valley Field Centre, opened in 1986, is the base for many scientific studies relating to tropical rainforest ecology.

as well as training and educational courses. The centre has been strong and successful for several reasons, not least the existence of an active, legally mandated management committee, and the long-standing support of both the Sabah Foundation and Britain's Royal Society. The INFAPRO programme, which actively restores logged forest with the intention of boosting carbon dioxide capture during the forest regeneration process, is described in the section on forest management units (see page 68). Another programme, which ran in the early 1990s and was funded by the Sabah Foundation and the New England Power Company of the USA, explored the possibility of reducing collateral damage caused during logging operations, to the extent that more young trees could be maintained and contribute to carbon capture.

ABOVE Leopard Cat (*Prionailurus bengalensis*), Sabah's commonest wild cat, and a species of forest edges that enters plantations to feed on rats.

LEFT Lesser Mousedeer (*Tragulus javanicus*), the smallest hoofed mammal, is a common resident of the flat lands and stream sides in Danum Valley.

Some of the early practical experiments in 'reduced-impact logging' in tropical evergreen rainforests were thus conducted in Ulu Segama. Various methods to reduce the adverse impacts of logging were tried, including identifying and marking trees that have to be retained as future crop trees, and imposing a fine on the contractor if they are felled or damaged; cutting lianas prior to felling commercial trees (on the theory that falling large trees draped with lianas tend to pull down other adjacent trees); training chainsaw operators to cut trees so that they will fall in a direction that will cause the least collateral damage; strictly prohibiting any logging activities near streams and rivers; building simple drains at an angle across abandoned log-hauling trails and roads to help divert rainwater into undisturbed leaf litter rather than streams; prohibiting bulldozer operators from driving onto steep slopes and from scraping soil with the front blade; prohibiting felling of trees on steep slopes; and stopping logging operations during wet weather.

Formal studies in Sabah and elsewhere produced analyses to show that such reduced-impact logging methods can also help to reduce logging costs. In ideal circumstances perhaps they can, but local contractors were not convinced. Two particular complaints from logging contractors in the Ulu Segama experiments were that they were permitted to extract significantly fewer trees per hectare under reduced-impact logging rules, and that the imposition of 'stop work' orders during wet spells caused a considerable loss of income for periods when, previously, they would have continued logging. Both complaints may be valid from the point of view of the contractors, but for society at large, reduced-impact logging has benefits. Use of heavy machinery such as bulldozers during rain certainly contributes to the amount of soil and rock particles washed into streams and rivers, and reducing the number of trees felled per hectare also reduces soil damage, impacts on water, and loss of the forest's structure, biodiversity and regeneration capacity.

A more recent innovative programme is the Malua BioBank, whereby the Sabah government has licensed conservation rights over the Malua Forest Reserve. A proportion of funds derived from the sales of so-called biodiversity conservation certificates are shared between the government (in return for agreeing to conserve the area for the next 50 years) and activities designed to help protect and rehabilitate this forest area.

Tabin

In the early 1880s, the British North Borneo Company engaged a young man called Frank Hatton to conduct mineral-prospecting explorations in eastern Sabah. When returning down the Segama River in March 1883, Hatton met with an accident while tracking a wounded elephant and died at the age of 22. His name is commemorated by Mount Hatton, the highest point in the Dent Peninsula, now in the middle of the Tabin Wildlife Reserve. Always struggling to stay afloat and pay for the administration of North Borneo, the company persisted in seeking minerals for its salvation. Thus, in 1936–39, geologists of the Royal Dutch Shell group made surveys in the Dent Peninsula, mainly seeking prospects for petroleum. In 1937, after travelling up the Tabin River for days and walking under forest shade, geologist Eduard Wenk reached one of the area's two largest mud volcanoes, now also in the middle of Tabin Wildlife Reserve, describing it thus:

Malay Civet (*Viverra tangalunga*), a nocturnal mammal common in logged forests.

following elephant foot prints we cut right through the underbrush and hit a vast, blindingly white opening. No vegetation, not even grass was growing. Only bleached rocks and salty mud existed. In the centre of the place a salt water spring with fresh elephant, as well as rhinoceros, deer, pig and wild cattle, tracks and many humming wasps called our attention. This was obviously a favourite meeting ground for all kinds of game. Some of the rhino footprints were very impressive. Imagine, the Chinese pay $450–500 for one rhino. The coolies planned to return to Ulu Tabin as soon as they had saved enough money for a shot gun and ball ammunition.

In the 1960s and 1970s, much of the primary rainforest of the Dent Peninsula was allocated to political leaders of the time as a means of raising funds for their activities. The only human settlements in the entire region, all small in extent, were at Tomanggong (with a mix of immigrants, including Ibans from Sarawak who had

found employment at the new Rivers Estate oil-palm plantation in the early 1960s), Tidong and Dagat (home to native Tidung people who migrated here from the Labuk River in 1952), along the eastern coast (settled by Bajau and Suluk people, who have affinities across the sea to the Philippines), on the lower Tungku River (inhabited by a mix of a minority native ethnic group, the Begahak, possibly the original 'Sabahans', along with descendents of traders from the heydays of the Sulu sultanate) and at Bakapit (housing Filipinos and a few Westerners working at the earliest logging operation in the area). The first commercial logging of the Dent Peninsula was rapid and comprehensive, with the bulk of it carried out between 1970 and 1985.

The first time I heard of Tabin was at a Christmas party in Sandakan in 1979, in the house built by American author and prisoner of war Agnes Keith and her husband, which was then being used – improbable though it may seem now – as accommodation for Canadian and Japanese volunteers working with the Forestry Department.

ABOVE Black-and-crimson Pitta (*Pitta ussheri*), formerly known as Garnet Pitta (*P. granatina*), a bird of dense undergrowth in lowland forests such as Tabin.

LEFT The Tabin River valley, stronghold for large mammals including elephants and Tembadau (wild cattle).

James Barrett, the son of the man who had pioneered development of an oil-palm plantation at Tomanggong in the early 1960s, told me that Bornean Rhinoceros were often sighted by men working in a logging concession in the Tagas-tagas and Tabin river catchments, within the Silabukan Commercial Forest Reserve. With assistant game rangers Rashid Saburi and Simon Ambi, we spent two weeks in March 1980 walking from the upper Tabin River to the Tabin mud volcano, north to Tagas-tagas and back to Lipad, the location of the current Tabin Wildlife Reserve headquarters. At Tagas-tagas we saw logs being transported out of the forest by locomotive to the Segama River, along one of the last such railways existing in Sabah. Finding evidence of several rhinos during this trip, and knowing that effective protection of them from hunters would be very difficult to enforce, the Sabah Forestry

Department and WWF-Malaysia made a recommendation to the International Union for Conservation of Nature and Natural Resources (IUCN) that these animals should be captured and translocated to a safer site. However, subsequent visits to the area in 1980–81 convinced us that the Bornean Rhinoceros could survive *in situ* if parts of the Silabukan and Lumerau commercial forest reserves could be retained as a refuge for them, with logging ceasing there.

Sunset at Tabin Wildlife Reserve, with Large Flying Foxes (*Pteropus vampyrus*), a fruit-eating bat with a wingspan of over 1m. Tabin is the largest protected forest in eastern Sabah and one of the most significant remaining tracts of lowland dipterocarp forest in the world. It is of great importance for Bornean lowland vertebrates.

This proposal was accepted, and the 120,000ha Tabin Wildlife Reserve came into existence in March 1984, formed from parts of the former commercial forest reserves and with an 8,000ha core area of virgin forest located around Mount Hatton.

For several reasons, Tabin has enjoyed less interest and fame than the other forest conservation areas in Sabah. It has no spectacular physical or geological features other than its large mud volcanoes, and no navigable rivers aside from the lower reaches of the remote Tabin River on its northern fringes. In addition, between 1984 and 2010, no formal research programme or other high-profile activity was carried out at Tabin.

At the time of writing, however, some significant changes to this situation were underway with the development of the Borneo Rhino Sanctuary, a programme that aims to concentrate in one area individuals of the critically endangered Bornean Rhinoceros, as a means to promote breeding. Senior Wildlife Veterinarian Dr Sen Nathan and Senior Ranger Herman Stawin of the Sabah Wildlife Department are working with NGOs and dedicated individuals to try to secure the future of this sub-species of the Sumatran Rhinoceros, with a special emphasis on Tabin.

For visiting naturalists, other features of interest include a diversity of lowland forest bird species, often more readily visible here in the broken forest canopy of the formerly logged forest than at other sites. Sightings can usually also be obtained of Bearded Pigs, Leopard Cats (*Prionailarus bengalensis*), civets and other wildlife species when these animals venture out of the forest into adjacent oil-palm plantation to feed at night, and there is a small chance of encounters with more spectacular species such as the Borneo Elephant, Sun Bear and Bornean Clouded Leopard. In addition, there is one readily accessible large mud volcano in the reserve.

Limestone Caves

Limestone outcrops of various sizes dot Sabah's landscape south of the Labuk River, especially in the eastern lowlands. Caves in the limestone have biological, historical and archaeological interest. Sarawak Museum's curator, Tom Harrisson, and his wife Barbara explored some of the sites in the 1960s, and in their 1971 book *The Prehistory of Sabah* described how the caves represent part of a web of human links that dates back to the early 15th century, if not earlier. Later research has shown that humans have

intermittently inhabited the Baturong caves, and presumably at least some other caves, for at least 28,000 years. A genus of small birds commonly known as cave swiftlets and scientifically as *Aerodramus* (formerly *Collocalia*) occurs in the region between the Andaman Islands and New Caledonia. These swiftlets do not perch

on branches or wires, but instead cling only to the surfaces of caves, rocks or buildings. The most prominent feature of the birds is that they echolocate in the darkness of caves, meaning that they emit fast clicking sounds whose echoes provide them with a picture of what is in front of them as they fly.

Gomantong limestone hill, located on the northern fringes of the Kinabatangan floodplain, contains caves that provides roosting sites for perhaps 2 million bats and a million or so cave swiflets.

Two species of swiftlets make nests that are gathered to obtain the main ingredient of the prized Chinese delicacy of bird's-nest soup. That ingredient is the swiftlets' own saliva, which is exuded as sticky, protein-rich, translucent strands, and fashioned in the form of a tiny stretched handkerchief attached to the walls of the caves, to form a pouch-like nest in which eggs are laid. The Edible-nest Swiftlet (*Aerodramus fuciphagus*) makes its nest on cave walls from its own solidified saliva, while the Black-nest Swiftlet (*Aerodramus maximus*) makes its nest from both saliva and its own feathers. Exactly how or when the saliva was first used as an edible product by the Chinese remains unknown, but most likely there is some connection between the nests, the caves, indigenous human inhabitants of eastern Sabah and early Chinese contacts with Borneo. In the early 1400s, the Ming government of China sent out seven naval expeditions to the Southeast Asian and Indian region, led by Zheng He. Although it is not certain that these expeditions reached Sabah, legends exist of contacts and intermarriage between Chinese sailors and locals along the Kinabatangan River.

The largest and most famous limestone outcrop of eastern Sabah is the 230m-high Gomantong, located on the northern fringes of the Kinabatangan floodplain and reached via a junction off the Sukau–Sandakan road. Gomantong is of particular interest for its caves, which are estimated to be the roosting site of some 2 million bats and a million or so swiftlets, including both the Edible-nest and Black-nest species. There are also features of historical and ecological interest within the caves, but the sloping terrain and thick guano on the cave floors create conditions unsuitable for the preservation of fossils and human remains, so the archaeological history of the site is unknown.

In Gomantong, the swiftlet nests are gathered according to an organised schedule that allows two harvests each year, which ensures that the birds will not become extinct.

ABOVE A closer view of the outside of Gomantong limestone hill.

OPPOSITE Two species of swiftlets (*Aerodramus* species) make nests that are harvested for making bird's-nest soup, according to a schedule that allows the birds to rear young annually, by men using ladders and ropes of rattan, wood and bamboo.

One harvest is collected just before the bulk of the swiftlets have nearly completed making their nests and before eggs are laid. The birds then construct a replacement nest, which is used to lay eggs and rear the young. After the young are able to fly, some seven or eight months after the initial nest construction, the used nests are harvested. Methods of collecting the nests were developed hundreds of years ago and remain much the same. These include the use of long, flexible ladders and ropes, long poles and tiny lamps.

LEFT A nest of the Black-nest Swiftlet (*Aerodramus maximus*), constructed from the birds' own feathers, cemented together by its saliva, the latter being extracted for human consumption.

BELOW Bat Hawks (*Macheiramphus alcinus*), which prey on swiftlets and bats as they leave Gomantong caves.

In the late afternoon, the swiftlets – which feed on the wing during the day on tiny insects – return to the caves to roost overnight. Just before dusk, the bats emerge from the caves, in swirling masses, to feed on nocturnal flying insects. With such large numbers of swiftlets and bats passing in and out of the caves daily, and deaths of both types of these animals from old age and disease, it is not surprising that predators and scavengers have evolved to take advantage of this guaranteed food source. In the open air, these include Bat Hawks (*Macheiramphus alcinus*), as well as other raptors and even hornbills. Positioning themselves on bushes around the cave mouths, snakes snatch emerging bats. Most obvious of all, however, are the myriads of cockroaches, scutigerid centipedes and other specialist invertebrates that live permanently inside the caves to feed on fallen bats and swiftlets and their infants and eggs.

Gomantong and several smaller limestone outcrops in lower Kinabatangan, their caves and rights over the edible nests were seized by the British in the early years of the North Borneo administration. In the case of Gomantong, this resulted in the death by shooting in 1884 of the head of Melapi village (immediately upstream from the mouth of the Menanggul River and now a part of Sukau). In contrast, rights over collection of swiftlet nests from the next largest limestone outcrop and cave system in Sabah, at Madai (off the Lahad Datu–Tawau road), are vested in the Idahan community.

Kinabatangan Floodplain: Corridor of Life

The Kinabatangan is Sabah's largest river, with a total catchment size of nearly a quarter of the state's entire land area. The lowest parts of the river meander across a floodplain, where muddy waters overflow the banks during rainy periods, bringing immediate damage but also longer-term fertility to the swampy, oxygen-starved soils. Owing to a combination of commercial logging (which started in the 1950s and stopped only at the end of the 20th century), fire escaping from plantations developed in the 1980s and 1990s, and attempts to grow oil palm in swamps, much of the original Kinabatangan floodplain forest has gone or is badly degraded. Nevertheless, the lower Kinabatangan is probably now the only large river system in Southeast Asia that still has significant tracts of natural forest along its banks, as well as in the freshwater swamps behind the banks. Seasonally flooded forests such as this are known as *varzea* in the Amazon, but there is no local equivalent name in the Malaysian languages.

Wildlife in the lower Kinabatangan

For naturalists, the lower Kinabatangan's combination of a large river, smaller tributaries and lakes and the floodplain offer a unique opportunity to view the area's scenery, trees and wildlife from a boat. There is hardly a need to walk, but if one chooses to do so, it is on flat land, rather than on the endless slopes that predominate in

Kinabatangan floodplain represents one of the most significant global habitats for Storm's Stork (*Ciconia stormi*), a species of Borneo, Sumatra and Peninsular Malaysia.

ABOVE Blue-eared Kingfisher (*Alcedo meninting*), a species of forested swamps and small tributaries off the main Kinabatangan River.

RIGHT Oriental Darter (*Anhinga melanogaster*), a bird that catches fish by diving into Kinabatangan River and oxbow lakes.

much of Sabah. The lower Kinabatangan is most famous for offering the chance to see, during the daytime, large mammals such as Proboscis Monkeys, Bornean Orangutans and Borneo Elephants, and resident waterbirds such as the Oriental Darter (*Anhinga melanogaster*) and Storm's Stork (*Ciconia stormi*). For birders, the area probably offers the best prospect, along with the Danum Valley (see above), for a sighting of the elusive Bornean Ground-cuckoo, a specialist of flat riverside forest land. A boat cruise at night, meanwhile, provides potential sightings of the Buffy Fish-owl (*Ketupa ketupu*) and wild cats. For keen visitors who spend some of their time on land in the lower Kinabatangan, there are other distinctive, much smaller wildlife species of interest, even close to the tourist lodges. These include the Least Pygmy Squirrel (*Exilisciurus exilis*), one of the world's smallest squirrels, which periodically makes fast runs along branches and tree trunks in search of food, as well as 5cm-long pill millipedes walking on the leaf litter, and gliding lizards.

Significance of the Kinabatangan floodplain

Some of the remaining scattered forest patches in the Kinabatangan floodplain are examples of a habitat type that is now extremely rare globally: natural vegetation of an alluvial floodplain. This is a habitat that was once widespread in Southeast Asia but, starting thousands of years ago, has gradually been converted to rice paddies. The ability of certain varieties of rice to grow in flooded land, where few tree species can survive, was one of the contributory reasons why rice expanded as the major food crop throughout Southeast Asia. Until a few decades ago, the native Orang Sungai families of the lower Kinabatangan planted non-irrigated 'hill' rice on the raised alluvial riverside terrace, and small quantities of a long-stemmed variety of rice in natural swamps near their villages. Irrigated 'wet paddy' farming was introduced here only with government assistance in the 1970s, but it has remained unpopular, perhaps because rice is readily available in shops, and growing oil palms, as well as other economic opportunities, are more attractive to local residents.

In South Kalimantan, at the southern end of Borneo, both the culture and population of the Banjar people expanded centuries ago following the conversion of the massive Barito River floodplain to wet paddy. In light of this, it is unclear why the lower Kinabatangan largely escaped extensive human settlement and similar agricultural conversion. In the 19th century, the British administration of North Borneo thought that piracy from the southern Philippines and head-hunting raids from Kalimantan were the main reasons for the very

172

small numbers of human inhabitants of the lower Kinabatangan. Diseases certainly took a large toll on communities from time to time, but the same occurred elsewhere. More likely, the unpredictable timing and depth of flooding, compared to that generated by the more seasonal rainfall patterns on much of mainland Asia, made the growing of wet paddy very risky in the high but erratic rainfall zone of northern Borneo.

Floodplains are not a stable ecosystem. The interplay of changing water volume, speed of water flow, and attrition and redeposition of sediments means that the river's course changes slowly but inevitably. Along the course of the Kinabatangan River are more than a dozen oxbow lakes (known locally as *danau*), the remnants of former river bends that were cut off by natural erosion and deposition of riverside silt. Some of the oxbow lakes retain thin connections of water channels to the main river, making them accessible by small boat.

OPPOSITE ABOVE Buffy Fish Owls (*Ketupa ketupu*), the most commonly seen owl in riverside forests in the Kinabatangan floodplain, feed on a forest rat.

BELOW Abai village, at the mouth of Kinabatangan River. The historically sparse human population of Kinabatangan floodplain may be due in part to the unpredictable timing and severity of floods, which make rice cultivation a risky basis for long-term settlement.

OVERLEAF Near the mouth of Kinabatangan River, a juxtaposition of Nipah Palms (near the water's edge, left side), Sonneratia Mangrove (right), Nibong Palms (very tall with pale trunks) and transitional forest (*Cerbera* tree with white flowers).

A few of the lakes are still quite deep, but most are in the process of slowly filling with silt and becoming covered with sedges and small trees. On the north side of the Kinabatangan, opposite the Tenegang Besar River halfway between Sukau and Bilit villages, for example, is a small oxbow lake that was a bend in the main river until, according to old residents, a great flood cut through it one night around 1952. For some reason, this lake, almost never visited, has filled up quickly, but other such lakes seem to have barely changed for more than 50 years. A research and training centre has been established at Danuau Girang, while visits to the lakes near Sukau and Abai are included in some nature tours.

Conservation of the Kinabatangan

The Kinabatangan represents a classic story of how real-life conservation operates, a story that will take another few decades to reach at least some degree of completion. During my first year in Sabah, in 1979–80, I was told repeatedly by a whole range of people with different backgrounds and interests that it was 'too late' to bother with the lower Kinabatangan, based on the observations that all the forests had by then been logged and most of the land already allocated by government policy for agriculture. Thus, the lower Kinabatangan was omitted from the list of areas surveyed under the state-wide faunal survey conducted in 1979–81. Misgivings over abandoning the region to near-total conversion to agriculture built up in subsequent years. For a start, land suitability maps prepared in the 1970s already showed that the lower Kinabatangan was a complex patchwork of soils, ranging from sites ideal for permanent cultivation to those deemed unsuitable for any kind of exploitative use owing to constant waterlogging and periodic flooding.

OPPOSITE The estuary of Kinabatangan River consists of vast tracts of mangrove and Nipah forests that stretch westwards to Sandakan and eastwards to the mouth of the Segama River.

BELOW Between sunset and dusk on the Kinabatangan River near Sukau.

OVERLEAF Dusk (depicted here) and dawn represent the most magical times to be in a boat on the Kinabatangan River, as both colours and the array of insect sounds and bird calls change. At dusk, sounds become much more subdued, as cicadas give way to crickets, and almost all bird calls cease. The sound of water lapping on the boat seems suddenly louder.

TOP Hooded Pitta (*Pitta sordida*), one of four resident pitta species that occur in the dense forests of the lower Kinabatangan area.

PREVIOUS PAGE
Fortunate visitors to Kinabatangan River may see a herd of elephants travelling and feeding on the riverbank, most often after mid-afternoon or before mid-morning. As land use patterns stabilise in the Kinabatangan floodplain, the resident elephant population will provide long-term challenges for wildlife managers, especially in how to minimise conflict when elephants enter and feed in villages and plantations.

In 1983, I visited the Menanggul River just as construction of the new road to Sukau was approaching the village, and was captivated by the tranquillity of the area as well as the abundance of birdlife and Proboscis Monkeys. I was also fascinated by the fact that the river has its headwaters on the slopes of the Gomantong limestone hill (see above) and then runs through an extensive peat swamp – hence the dark blackish colour of its waters. In days gone by, hardy Orang Sungai and natives from what is now the southern Philippines must not only have risked their lives collecting nests from the Gomantong caves, but also spent days ferrying them on rafts or dugout canoes down the Menanggul River to Melapi (Sukau) to await the arrival of traders from Sulu.

Also in 1983, a state-wide survey of crocodiles showed that the greatest numbers at that time were in the lower Kinabatangan. And from field surveys conducted in 1985–87, it became apparent that the greatest local concentrations of orang-utans in Malaysian Borneo, as well as of elephants and Oriental Darters, were in the heavily logged forests of the area. It was also during this period that it became clear that the claim by many biologists that heavily logged forests were 'useless' for wildlife was in error. But by this time, the process of issuing titles to land for the development of plantations throughout most of the lower Kinabatangan was well advanced. It seemed that the arguments for conservation were sound, but had been voiced too late.

By 1989, however, several things had changed. Prospects for nature tourism in Sabah were becoming more apparent, with a few hardy souls venturing to take foreigners to see Proboscis Monkeys at Sukau and near Batu Putih. The new Sabah Wildlife Department had been established in 1988, and placed under the purview of a ministry where environment and tourism portfolios had been combined. In 1989, the Permanent Secretary to the Ministry of Tourism and Environmental Development, Datuk Wilfred Lingham, felt that arguing for a Kinabatangan wildlife sanctuary on the basis of tourism, rather than conservation, might be attractive to the government. The idea was to preserve forest cover along the banks of the lower Kinabatangan River, thereby retaining habitat for breeding populations of all the native wildlife species, while at the same time allowing visitors to see the wildlife from boats – an opportunity that was clearly unique in Malaysia.

BELOW With males growing to 5m in length, the Estuarine Crocodile (*Crocodylus porosus*) is the world's largest living reptile species. Numbers appear to have increased in the Kinabatangan and other rivers in Sabah over the past few decades.

The idea was right, but the initial proposal for the sanctuary attracted much opposition. Many thousands of landowners and would-be landowners were affected by the proposal. Some local people were worried that their ancestral lands would be taken from them, while oil-palm plantation developers expressed concern over losing potential land. Land speculators and brokers added to the voices against a Kinabatangan wildlife sanctuary. Even some conservation biologists felt that it would be of limited value because of the degraded nature of the forest, and its long, thin shape, which allowed plenty of access for encroachers. Eventually a compromise was reached and approved by the Sabah government in 1994. The resulting Kinabatangan Wildlife Sanctuary was formed by retaining more than 20 blocks of forest, separated by rivers, plantations, roads and villages. By good fortune, tracts of forest had been retained as forest reserve since the British administration around all the limestone outcrops in the lower Kinabatangan that contain caves. Thus, the current extent and partial continuity of natural vegetation in the lower Kinabatangan is formed by a combination of protected forests – wildlife sanctuary under the purview of the Sabah Wildlife Department, and forest reserves under the purview of the Sabah Forestry Department.

Barring major disasters, the majority of wild species found in the lower Kinabatangan can probably survive in the long term with the maintenance and, where necessary, restoration of habitats in the current array of protected forests. For a few species, however, the fact that the protected areas are fragmented, are individually small in size and lack large old trees will increasingly present problems to their long-term survival. The chief concerns are elephants (which are forced to travel through plantations and even villages to move from one area to another), orang-utans (which are confined to forest blocks that may not supply enough food, and which will suffer from inbreeding if they cannot move to seek mates in other blocks) and hornbills (which need holes in old, mature trees for nesting). A major challenge now

OPPOSITE ABOVE White-crowned Hornbills (*Aceros comatus*), a species that tends to be active around sunset.

OPPOSITE BELOW Swamp Mallotus or Salungapit (*Mallotus muticus*) trees dominate the Kinabatangan floodplain forest on the most waterlogged sites, especially in old oxbow lakes filled with clay sediment.

and for the coming years is to re-establish, as far as is reasonably possible, continuity of natural vegetation from the mouth of the Kinabatangan River up to the central parts of Sabah, as well as encourage an overall increase and improvement in forest cover. In practice, complete continuity will never be possible, especially where there are old established villages such as Sukau and where there are major public roads. For large wildlife species, more connectivity of natural habitats is better than less, but complete connectivity of closed-canopy forest is not essential. In fact, we tend to assume that wild species are less tenacious or adaptable than they are in reality. Just one mature male of a species such as the Borneo Elephant or Bornean Orang-utan, crossing a river or road every 10 years, can help to spread and maintain genetic diversity in small populations.

A combination of natural regeneration and active reafforestation efforts since the late 1990s, by local and non-governmental groups assisted by the Sabah Forestry Department, has set the Kinabatangan floodplain on a slow course towards a more ecologically balanced pattern of land use. One of the lessons learned through this active restoration work is that floods are likely to kill the majority of seedlings planted on flood-prone lands, even those of specialist floodplain tree species. Tall seedlings and cuttings of certain tree species can be used, but this is laborious and costly work. For the most flood-prone sites, it may be best just to allow a natural vegetation regeneration process to take place.

As with most kinds of research into tropical rainforest ecosystems, each new observation and conclusion tends to raise as many new questions as it answers. Up to the 1980s, flood-prone lands in the Kinabatangan bore quite a diversity of tree species, with only the very wettest sites supporting stands of one species such as *Mallotus muticus*. So the question arises, how did the original forest develop on flood-prone land in the face of flooding events that were unpredictable in both their timing and severity? Some people believe that there are more or worse floods in the Kinabatangan now than in the past, but that seems unlikely. Old records reveal that there were indeed periodic massive floods before the era of logging and plantations. What seems to have changed – although there are insufficient records to be sure – is that floodwaters tend to rise more quickly now than in the past, and that their timing is less clustered around the northern monsoon season than it once was.

The redevelopment of a diverse forest on the Kinabatangan would probably take at least a century, even with human assistance in replanting. Possibly, random periods of several contiguous years without a major flood would represent the best window of opportunity for the more flood-sensitive species to become re-established through active planting and by the dispersion of seeds by fruit bats, birds and the wind.

Oil palm grown on the floodplain requires drainage, to keep the plantation land from becoming waterlogged and to channel away waters during floods. This deliberate redirection of floodwater out of plantations and onto the remaining forest areas probably tends to lead to a process whereby flood-tolerant tree species continue to thrive, and these hardy species may tend to suppress the re-establishment of a diverse array of trees and strangling figs. Owners of land in the Kinabatangan floodplain who wish to aid the long-term conservation of wildlife species that require native tree cover can therefore make one or more of several possible contributions. One is to abandon the most waterlogged and flood-prone areas to nature, and even block some of the

drainage canals. The other is to replant parts of their land with native floodplain tree species. The chances are that, in the long run, when palm-oil prices are low and wood prices high, and they have the opportunity to cut some of the trees and sell the wood, landowners might not regret such action. Another option – perhaps carried out during the next replanting of over-mature oil palms – is to allocate relatively small areas of flood-free land, carefully chosen in the context of the overall Kinabatangan floodplain landscape, to restore a diverse tree cover.

The Heart of Sabah: Deramakot, Imbak Canyon and Telupid Forest Complex

A joint programme of the governments of Malaysian Borneo, Indonesian Borneo and Brunei Darussalam exists to work for trans-frontier collaboration in the protection and management of forests and other natural features. The programme is called Heart of Borneo, and a relatively large proportion of the heart lies in Sabah,

ABOVE Following heavy exploitation in the 1960s to 1980s, Deramakot's forests (left side in this picture) are now regenerating well under a sustainable management regime.

OPPOSITE Deramakot is one of the few established natural tropical timber production forests certified as sustainably managed under the rigorous Forest Stewardship Council standards.

encompassing the west coast mountains up to Mount Kinabalu, much of the state's interior, and some of the east coast lowland forests, which are of supreme importance for the conservation of wild Sabah's – and Borneo's – large mammals. The three areas described here have been chosen because they are located relatively close to one another in central Sabah, yet they also display some remarkable differences both in their biology and in their historical background.

Deramakot

One of Sabah's geographical features, hardly ever mentioned except in technical texts, is the Lokan peneplain, a seemingly endless maze of low sandstone and mudstone ridges divided by damp valleys of clay-rich soils. A peneplain is an extensive, generally low but dissected plain where the underlying rock has been folded and tilted by tectonic forces, and where an array of meandering streams has eroded the softer rocks over millions of years. The Lokan peneplain extends over an area of more than 250,000ha between the Labuk and Kinabatangan rivers, and between Telupid and the Sandakan Peninsula. In the early years of the British North Borneo Company, explorer Frank Hatton and Sandakan-based British Resident William Pryer entered parts of the region. Anyone walking through here at that time would soon become lost without a compass. In 1945, Australian

and British prisoners of war were forced by their Japanese captors to cross the region from Sandakan to Ranau on a series of death marches. Nowadays, the Sandakan–Kota Kinabalu highway passes through the middle of the peneplain, and over half of it is covered in oil palms on neat terraces that snake along the contours of the jumble of low hills and valleys.

Deramakot Forest Reserve covers about 20 per cent of the Lokan peneplain, and in most respects is unremarkable. The Deramakot River is tiny and, for newcomers, its name does not roll easily off the tongue. In 1956, Robert Inger spent four weeks here, leading an expedition to collect museum specimens of vertebrate animals of the lowland rainforests of Borneo. Fifty years on, Dr Inger was conferred the title of Dato by the government of Sarawak for his unique half-century of contributions to the study of Bornean frogs and reptiles.

The first time I heard of Deramakot was in 1983, when I quizzed a Filipino friend working for a logging company in Sandakan on whether he had ever come across a rhino. He told me that he had, while in a Land Rover being driven by a logging contractor in Deramakot in 1978. The rhino was ambling along the roadside, and they rammed it, killing it to obtain its valuable horns.

ABOVE Monitoring of wildlife populations (Bearded Pig footprints in roadside mud shown here) is a requirement in the Deramakot management plan.

LEFT Leeches in a salt-water spring in Deramakot Forest Reserve.

The story sounds shocking today, but in essence is no different from similar phases in the history of other countries, when the opening up of previously remote forests by pioneers had a fatal impact on the mammals that naturally occur there at low population densities. The Bornean Rhinoceros was already extremely rare in eastern Sabah by the time of independence in 1963. At the height of the logging era, the sheer number of roads, bulldozers and chainsaw operators scattered around the region meant that it was just a matter of time before most of the final stragglers became the target of poachers.

But for a decision in 1989 by the then Director of the Sabah Forestry Department, Datuk Miller Munang, to turn Deramakot into a model site for the development of sustainable forestry, this forest might never have become either famous or significant in proving that nature conservation and sustainable wood production can coexist in the same tropical evergreen rainforest area.

Commercial-scale logging started in Deramakot in the 1960s and continued full swing during the 1970s and 1980s. From the early 1990s, however, the Sabah Forestry Department, with technical support from the German Agency for Technical Cooperation (GTZ), developed a management system specifically aimed at generating sustainable production of timber from Sabah's logged forest lands. Deramakot was the first natural forest in Malaysia to be certified, in 1997, as sustainably managed under the stringent global Forest Stewardship Council (FSC) principles and criteria. Since the 1990s, timber trees have been cut at a rate that matches the natural regrowth of wood. The timber is auctioned every few months, generally fetching better than prevailing market prices. This system allows Deramakot to be run as a profitable, sustainable business.

Usually, heads of government around the world do not tend to be overly interested in forestry. But because of its unique features, Deramakot has been visited and praised by two of Malaysia's prime ministers. Unfortunately, the system cannot be replicated fully in all areas, because factors such as soil fertility, topography, remoteness and forest type all play important roles in determining whether a particular forest area can produce timber both sustainably and profitably.

Deramakot, together with parts of the adjacent Segaliud-Lokan and Tangkulap forest reserves, retains the last large tract of the lowland dipterocarp forest that once entirely covered the Lokan peneplain, once home to the Bornean Rhinoceros, Borneo Elephant, Bornean Orangutan, Tembadau, Sun Bears, Bornean Clouded Leopards and other large mammals. Although the last rhinoceros disappeared here around 1984, all the other species still remain as sizeable breeding populations. Indeed, surveys of Bornean Orang-utans show that Deramakot now sustains the highest population densities (that is, number of individuals per square kilometre) of the species anywhere in Malaysian Borneo. Long-term studies may possibly reveal that orang-utan population densities rise and fall over the years, in Deramakot and elsewhere, according to natural annual variations in fruit production, or to malaria or other factors. This would not be surprising, as it has long been known that wildlife populations in temperate habitats rise and fall according to natural environmental changes, irrespective of human influence. Despite a popular image of tropical rainforests as somehow more stable than temperate habitats, there is actually no good reason that they should be particularly stable from the perspective of wild animal populations. Annual differences in the pattern and amount of rainfall and fruit production, the fact that tropical trees may need a few years to regain the necessary nutrients from mineral-poor soils in order to produce flowers, and the plethora of natural diseases and parasites within the ecosystem together suggest that we should expect ebbs and flows in wildlife numbers. In fact, over the past few years Bornean Orang-utan population densities in Deramakot appear to have remained quite stable. Small differences in the annual estimates of orang-utan numbers at Deramakot are just as likely to be a result of 'random' factors – including differences in the weather on survey days, in the exact survey routes taken or in the survey staff – as well as pure luck. If the annual orang-utan survey results turn out to be similar year after year, this would tend to suggest that an actively managed logged lowland dipterocarp forest is an unusually stable ecosystem.

Imbak Canyon

The Imbak Canyon is the most recent large area of primary rainforest in Sabah to have been designated a protected area, through the removal in 2008 of about 16,750ha of forest from the Sabah Foundation forest concession. The 'canyon' is actually a long, broad valley, with a river, the Imbak, flowing west to east through it, and with two long, steep sandstone ridges on either side.

The 25km long Imbak Canyon, the most recent large area of primary rainforest in Sabah to have been designated a protected area, is a long, broad valley with two east–west aligned steep sandstone ridges on either side. Rising to 1,500m above sea level, the ridges are another sign, like Maliau Basin, of ancient massive geological collapses underground.

These ridges were designated in 1984 as virgin jungle reserves, to be excluded from logging, mainly because the very steep terrain would have made timber extraction costly, difficult and environmentally damaging. By adding the lower, flatter Imbak Valley between those ridges, a major new conservation area was created.

A distinctive characteristic of the Imbak Canyon forest is the abundance of the Red Kapur tree, as well as several other rare dipterocarps, including the highly endangered *Dipterocarpus elongatus*. Given its remote location and rather sandy soils, it is likely that the Imbak Canyon has never been settled or cultivated, and so the forests here are probably among the oldest and least disturbed in Sabah.

Telupid forest complex

As you drive along the middle section of the Kota Kinabalu–Sandakan highway, past the small town of Telupid, or southwards off the highway through oil-palm plantations to Deramakot, several forest-covered hill ranges are prominent. Of these, six are protection forest reserves and three are of particular interest.

The Bukit Taviu Forest Reserve is worth a visit because the highway passing through it provides views of what is probably the most accessible hill dipterocarp forest in Sabah. The reserve also preserves a portion of the route followed during the Second World War Sandakan death marches (see above). The other two areas of interest are the Bidu-bidu Hills and Tawai. Both of these forest reserves protect hills that are part of a long range of ultrabasic rock, stretching from Mount Silam (near Lahad Datu, at the junction of the main road into the Danum Valley), via Ulu Segama and Mount Danum, to the southern fringes of Mount Kinabalu. The flora on ultrabasic soils is distinctly different from that at the same altitudes on other soil types. Only a few species of dipterocarps are present, and some plant species – such as the Bangkau-bangkau tree (*Borneodendron aenigmaticum*) – are restricted exclusively to the ultrabasic soils of Sabah.

Unfortunately, the more accessible northern parts of Tawai were severely burned during the El Niño droughts of recent decades, but overall both it and the Bidu-bidu Hills form the largest tracts of accessible lowland and hill forest on ultrabasic soils in Sabah. It is unlikely either could ever be managed sustainably for wood production or for plantations owing to the odd nature of the soils. Instead, ultrabasic forests best function as catchment areas to protect the quality of downstream and surrounding water supplies.

The water of Imbak River is normally rather clear, as the entire catchment is protected under primary forest, but soil, tree trunks, branches and other vegetation are frequently washed from the prevailing steep slopes during heavy rain storms.

Sandakan: Sepilok, Offshore Islands, and the Eastern Coastal Wetlands and Kulamba

Sandakan

Sandakan has been named Sabah's 'Nature City' – an appropriate epithet, for the sheer variety of natural areas that lie within a few hours' journey of the town. On the hills behind it, and on the nearby island of Pulau Berhala, are examples of original heath forest, along with some fine regenerating secondary forests. Perhaps more remarkable still is the 148ha Sandakan Rainforest Park, also known as the Kebun Cina Amenity Forest Reserve, a relict patch of dipterocarp forest just a few kilometres from town. Despite the proximity of Sandakan, which was capital of North Borneo from 1883 until 1947, and the occurrence of brush fires around the area during the droughts of 1983, 1987 and 1998, this forest survived without formal protected status until 2007, when it was finally given legal protection as a forest reserve. Part of the interest of the park is both historical and botanical: the very first records and descriptions of more than 100 species of wild Bornean plants are based on specimens collected here or very near here. Most of the collections were made in 1920 by Filipino collector Maximo Ramos, and in 1921 by Manila-based American botanist Adolph Elmer. The site now serves as a recreational forest for local people, as well as being unique in Southeast Asia for its joint biodiversity conservation and historical significance.

My first day in Sandakan, in 1979, was hosted by the Assistant Chief Game Warden (later Director) of the Sabah Wildlife Department, Patrick Andau, who showed me the sights. This was some years before the nature tourism sector realised that this is one of the gateways to wild Sabah – the Sepilok Orang-utan Rehabilitation Centre (established in 1964) and Turtle Islands Park (established as a park in 1977, although turtle conservation work started in 1966) were receiving only a trickle of adventurous foreign visitors at that time.

Sandakan town centre – Sabah's 'Nature City' was originally a trading post of the Sulu sultanate, capital of British North Borneo from 1883–1942, and the principal conduit for export of Sabah's timber during the 1970s to 1980s.

The late 1970s was the peak of Sabah's logging era, when more than a million logs of massive dipterocarp trees – some trucked out of the forest by road, and others floated or barged from the Kinabatangan River and north side of the Dent Peninsula – were collected annually in the 'log ponds' in the sea off Tanah Merah. Looking down from Trig Hill, one could see these logs, ranging from 50cm to 2m in diameter, lined up like so many matchsticks before being loaded onto a never-ending queue of ships from Japan. The logs of some species of dipterocarp are 'floaters', preferred at that time for their ease of transportation in water and used mainly to make plywood. 'Sinkers', or dense hardwood species, had to be tied to floaters.

Sandakan is not only the name of the town, but also a bay and peninsula, the latter an extension of the Lokan peneplain (see above). The precise origins of the name (meaning 'to be pawned' in the Sulu language) and of human settlement in the area are unknown. The earliest existing written record is by John Hunt, who apparently either visited or obtained contemporary information on Sandakan around 1812 during his trade-seeking tour of the southern Philippines, and who stated that the Sulu sultan Sharaf ud-Din appointed his son to govern the settlement of Sandakan from 1791 to 1808. He wrote further that Sandakan had a

> chief named tuan Abandool and a hundred Islams and there are many orang idan [natives] in the interior parts. Its annual products, when the Sulo people come over in numbers and chuse to exert themselves are 50 piculs [about 3 tonnes] of white birds' nest, 200 piculs [about 12 tonnes] of black ... 3 piculs of camphor ... 3 piculs of wax ... pearls ... and tripang [sea cucumbers].

This report provides fascinating links to the history of wild Sabah. The volume of birds' nests harvested from Gomantong caves nowadays is roughly 3.5 tonnes per year for white nests, and about 7 tonnes per year for black nests. Assuming that the bulk of nests harvested both in the early 1800s and today, two centuries later, come from Gomantong and pass through Sandakan, then annual production of white nests has remained remarkably similar, while production of black nests has declined, but by less than 50 per cent. Seemingly, the retention of forest around limestone caves and the strict government policy of regulating the harvesting of nests at Gomantong has had the desired outcome of preserving swiftlet populations in the Kinabatangan and Sandakan regions.

Also mentioned in Hunt's narrative is camphor, a constituent of the whitish resin of *Dryobalanops* trees, which would have been harvested by native people and carried in rattan rucksacks to villages along the Kinabatangan River for sale to Sulu traders. Wax was obtained from the nests of wild honey bees, and trade in this commodity became significant after the arrival of the Spanish in the northern Philippines in the 16th century. The New World (America), which the Spanish were colonising at the same time, lacked native honey bees, yet the Catholic Church used only beeswax to make candles. The cross-Pacific trade that developed between Manila in the Philippines and Acapulco in Mexico included wax, which would largely have originated from the extensive forests of eastern Sabah.

Wild honey bees in Sabah normally make their nests in the upper branches of the Mengaris tree. Native people throughout Borneo traditionally harvested the honey bee nests, as the honey and bee larvae were a locally consumed delicacy and the wax a source of trade income. However, only a very few brave souls conducted the actual harvesting. The method was similar throughout Borneo. A ladder reaching up near to the nest was fashioned into the tree trunk using sharpened Borneo Ironwood or bamboo pegs, hammered into the trunk, and with the outer ends of the pegs lashed together with split rattan canes. Following a ritual to provide protection from falls and bee stings, the harvester would ascend the ladder at night-time, bearing a knife attached to a pole, a smoke-producing fireball, a large container and a long rattan rope. The smoke would cause the bees to leave their nest, while the darkness would ensure that they would be disoriented and unable to attack the nest-collector. The harvester would then sling the rope over a branch and tie it to the container, filling the latter with chunks cut from the nest and lowering it slowly to the ground.

Sepilok

In 1879, William Pryer set foot on the north side of Sandakan Bay as the newly appointed British Resident, employed by the founders of the British North Borneo Company to develop eastern Sabah. At that time, the most remarkable feature of the region was its exceedingly small human population. Pryer was an energetic visionary, who dreamed that a century hence the perimeter of Sandakan Bay would be a metropolis, supported

Sepilok Orang-Utan Rehabilitation Centre started in 1964 as a simple project to rehabilitate immature orang-utans kept illegally as pets, but by the 1980s had become an unintended nature tourism icon.

by agriculture in the hinterlands. Early British administrators realised that, as agricultural expansion proceeded, so the forest would disappear from the Sandakan region, bringing with it the need for a specific forest area to be set aside to provide long-term wood supplies for Sandakan town. Thus, the Kabili-Sepilok Forest Reserve (usually known just as Sepilok) was established, the first part in 1931 and then an extra portion in 1938. Aside from supplying wood to Sandakan, it was a convenient site to conduct research into the management of dipterocarp forests. Selective logging was eventually phased out in the Sepilok forest in 1957.

The World Wildlife Fund (now called the Worldwide Fund for Nature, or WWF) was founded in 1961 to help save endangered species. In 1962, the international conservation organisation sent Barbara Harrisson, wife of anthropologist and ecologist Tom Harrisson, to British North Borneo to investigate the status of Bornean Orang-utans. She reported that the species was endangered (in fact, at that time, it was not) and that the main threat to

its survival was capture of young ones as pets (which was, in fact, trivial at that time). During a return visit two years later to the recently independent Sabah, and in collaboration with Assistant Chief Game Warden Stanley De Silva, Harrisson helped to establish the Sepilok Orang-utan Rehabilitation Centre, where pet orang-utans could be received and trained for a life back in the wild. The site was chosen because, in 1964, it was considered quite remote yet lay only just beyond the end of the main road out of Sandakan.

By 1970, as Sabah's timber boom got underway and many people saw how rich they could become simply by obtaining a logging licence, buying a bulldozer and cutting down large trees, Sepilok came under threat. This was averted by providing the interested party with an alternative logging site. As the years went by, the Kabili-Sepilok Forest Reserve became isolated by farm and plantation development. Road access to what is now the rehabilitation centre was completed in 1976 and, soon after, Sabah's first active inbound tour operator opened for business. The last visit to the western edge of Sepilok by a wild elephant herd from the Segaliud River occurred in 1980. By 1982, Sepilok had become cut off from the main forest blocks further inland. As Sandakan's human population expanded, the town's water supply, derived from boreholes, became inadequate.

It was decided that additional boreholes had to be opened to boost supplies, and plans were made to drill 17 new holes inside Sepilok. Fortunately, an alternative option was proposed, which involved piping water in large quantities directly from the Kinabatangan River, and the threat was averted.

In the 1980s, the availability of regular and moderately priced air routes from Europe all the way to Sandakan, coupled with road access to Sepilok, increasingly drew tourists to visit the Sepilok Orang-utan Rehabilitation Centre. The nature tourism element of Sepilok was never planned in the early years, but as the popularity of the site

ABOVE The Rainforest Discovery Centre represents one of Sabah's best lowland forest birding sites, notable for its resident group of endemic Bornean Bristleheads (*Pityriasis gymnocephala*).

LEFT The lake at Rainforest Discovery Centre on the northern edge of Sepilok Forest Reserve. The Centre includes a plant discovery garden with thousands of labelled tropical plants, well-designed discovery trails through the forest, a sturdy canopy walkway providing views within and above the tree canopy, and an exhibition hall.

grew, government authorities realised that it was not only an unintended yet ready-made tourism icon, but also a convenient way to attract and maintain interest in nature conservation, both locally and globally. As early as 1980, the first nature education centre had been established at Sepilok, with assistance from the government of Canada.

The first part of 1983 brought the brunt of a major El Niño drought to eastern Sabah. Almost no rain fell between August 1982 and May 1983, making this the worst drought in Borneo since 1915–16. Sepilok saw not only the first recorded case of large dipterocarp trees shedding most of their leaves, but also a boost in the

197

number of orang-utans being brought in, emaciated and dehydrated, just as the big wave of oil-palm plantation establishment was getting underway in eastern Sabah. By the mid-1980s, the role of Sepilok as a permanent orang-utan centre had been established by historical events and trends. Young orang-utans were coming in steadily as plantation expansion proceeded. The centre was advertised worldwide as a reason to visit Sabah, and the Bornean Orang-utan became the state's second big icon after Mount Kinabalu.

Now, in the 21st century, the number of orang-utans being brought to Sepilok is in decline, as patterns of land use stabilise. At some time in the future, Sepilok might not necessarily be the best place to see orang-utans in the forest, but it will remain the most convenient place for visitors who lack the time to go to other wild forest sites in eastern Sabah.

What has emerged since the turn of the 21st century is that Sepilok is a unique place for other reasons. Where else can you take a half-hour drive from a bustling town (Sandakan) to a well-kept example of Borneo's lowland diptercarp forest? Here, you can see, close up, centuries-old specimens of the famous Borneo Ironwood tree, which started life long before the first Europeans set foot on Sabah's soil. And at the Rainforest Discovery Centre you can make a quick, safe climb up into the forest canopy, where you have the chance to see what is Borneo's arguably most iconic bird species, the Bornean Bristlehead (*Pityriasis gymnocephala*). Even if that bird does not make a showing, there will be tens of other species on view, ranging from the spectacular hornbills to parakeets and broadmouths, and to diminutive spiderhunters, sunbirds and flowerpeckers. In the evening, Red Giant Flying Squirrels (*Petaurista petaurista*) may be seen in the Rainforest Discovery Centre, while at night the Western Tarsier emerges.

Offshore islands

Several islands lie within easy reach of Sandakan. Pulau Berhala and Pulau Libaran are the closest, but the Turtle Islands (Pulau Penyu) are the most famous, long established as a conservation area for Green Turtles (*Chelonia mydas*) and Hawksbill Turtles (*Eretmochelys imbricata*), and part of a cluster of islands that straddles the Malaysia and Philippines maritime border. The significance of these islands lies in the fact that their coral-sand beaches are the region's main egg-laying site for both of these marine turtle species.

Further north, off the mouth of the Sugut River, is the Sugut Islands Marine Conservation Area (SIMCA), consisting of the three islands of Pulau Lankayan, Pulau Billean and Pulau Tegaipil, and covering more than 46,000ha of sea. One unusual aspect of SIMCA is that it was established as a 'conservation area' under a section of the Sabah Wildlife Conservation Enactment 1997, which allows any kind of land – including private land –

to be managed at the direction of government for conservation purposes. This piece of legislation is unique in Malaysia, and SIMCA was the first site to be established by law as a conservation area rather than as a wildlife sanctuary, state park or forest reserve. Another unusual aspect of SIMCA is that management of the entire area has been delegated, under formal agreement and supervision, to private enterprise. In return for protecting and conserving the area, the operator is permitted to use SIMCA for nature tourism. Aside from providing visitors the chance to see marine turtles, these islands offer excellent snorkelling and diving.

Selingan, 40km north of Sandakan town, one of three islands in Turtle Islands Park, established in 1977 to protect nesting beaches for marine turtles.

The eastern coastal wetlands and Kulamba

Stretching northwards from Sandakan almost as far as the Bengkoka Peninsula, around Sandakan Bay and then eastwards along the northern side of the Dent Peninsula are Malaysia's largest tracts of mangrove and Nipah Palm forests. As nurseries and shelter for a variety of marine fisheries, these mangroves to a large extent account for Sandakan's traditional image as the seafood capital of Malaysia. As is the case globally, Sabah's coastal marine fisheries have taken a beating from many decades of intensive fishing, but Sandakan is still renowned for its fish and seafood, and living proof that retention of extensive wild areas – in this case mangroves – can serve economic purposes. In 2008, the mangrove, Nipah and associated coastal wetlands from Sandakan Bay to the eastern fringe of the Tabin Wildlife Reserve (see page 159) were designated under the Ramsar Convention (an international agreement that aims to ensure wetlands are conserved and used wisely) as a globally significant wetland, known as the Lower Kinabatangan-Segama Wetlands. The mangroves in the deltas of the Sugut and Labuk rivers are equally massive, and are protected from destruction or overexploitation as forest reserves.

Within this eastern coastal wetland region, the Kulamba Wildlife Reserve has a special role. In terms of forest and biodiversity conservation, this reserve contains the largest remaining extent – both in Malaysia and on the island of Borneo – of an intact coastal freshwater wetland with a variety of freshwater-swamp forest types, as well as patches of lowland dipterocarp forest on sites raised well above sea-level. Unlike the clay-rich freshwater-swamp forests of the Kinabatangan floodplain (see page 172), the Kulamba area is more sandy, and so has a rather different array of plant species. In terms of wildlife, Kulamba ranks fourth after Ulu Segama Malua-Danum, Deramakot-Segaliud-Lokan-Tangkulap and the Tabin Wildlife Reserve in terms of numbers of Bornean Orang-utans within a contiguous forest area.

Kulamba is, however, most famous for its Tembadau population. Long the target of hunters, this species of wild cattle has been persecuted for many decades at other sites. The lack of road access into Kulamba, along with an absence of rivers and clean freshwater supplies, has meant that hunters here are forced to seek their quarry by boat, and then either wade through deep swamps or wait on the sandy beach fringing the northern tip of the wildlife reserve at a point known as Tanjung Linsang.

Kulamba is periodically hit by fires – some set by would-be hunters – when long dry spells cause a drop in the reserve's water table to well below ground level. The worst such fire occurred in 1987, when a patch of more than 2,000ha out of Kulamba's total of 21,000ha was completely burned, and was subsequently replaced by natural regeneration with grasses, sedges, ferns and shrubs. Normally, such fires are anathema to anyone concerned with the conservation of tropical forests and endangered wildlife. In this case, however, there was a benefit: the Tembadau now have a massive grazing area secure within a legislated wildlife reserve.

OPPOSITE Green Turtle (*Chelonia mydas*) making a hole in the sand in which to lay her eggs; this is always done at night.

RIGHT Most of Sabah's mainland coastline north of Sandakan consists of vast mangrove forests representing the estuaries of the Sugut and Labuk rivers.

BELOW Selingan beach in the day time.

Final Thoughts

Probably no other location in Asia has such a diversity of wild and natural areas within a single state as Sabah, and with most of those areas accessible in under a day from a town. No wild species of plant or animal appears to have become extinct in recent historical times here, and only the Bornean Rhinoceros is now at crisis level. For species like the Malayan Tapir and Javan Rhinoceros, which went extinct in prehistoric times, the cause is likely to have been related to natural changes in land area and vegetation type after the end of the last ice age.

Climate change may now start to bring massive changes to wild Sabah, as elsewhere around the world, but in the meantime four main factors contribute to the sustenance of the state's range of natural biological diversity. The first of these is that about half the land area is under forest cover, including some significant lowland sites. A large proportion of these forests lie within the so-called Heart of Borneo area, contiguous with natural forest cover southwards into Central and West Kalimantan. Second, examples of all the original natural vegetation types are now included in Sabah's array of forest reserves, parks and wildlife sanctuaries. Third, a programme of habitat restoration is already underway in some of the most damaged lowland forests that are of particular importance to wildlife. Finally, the absence of both significant poverty and of international traffickers in wildlife products has, to date, kept the overexploitation of wild species at bay.

The forests of the Maliau Basin and Imbak Canyon, most of the Tawau Hills and Kinabalu Park, and the central part of Tabin around Mount Hatton are truly wild, with no evidence of any significant human disturbance, past or present. Peripheral parts of the Crocker Range, Danum Valley and Sepilok have experienced small degrees of human use in the past, but are still essentially natural areas, containing fine examples of montane, dipterocarp and heath forests. Most of the logged areas within Sabah's forest reserves have been damaged by the industry, and in some areas also by fire, but many are regenerating, either through slow natural processes or with human help. Some of the logged lowland forests contain Borneo's and Southeast Asia's largest remaining contiguous and relatively secure populations of the Bornean Orang-utan, Borneo Elephant, Tembadau, Bornean Clouded Leopard and Sun Bear.

The state also has some of the region's largest areas of mangrove forest, as well as a variety of coastal and freshwater-swamp forests. The Kinabatangan floodplain is special in that it sustains examples of freshwater-swamp forests on alluvial soils, which elsewhere in Asia have been converted to rice paddies.

Last but not least, Sabah is equally significant for its marine life, offshore islands and coral reefs. The Sulu Sea off the eastern side of the state forms the western fringe of the Coral Triangle region. As with terrestrial ecosystems, global climate change may have great consequences for these marine ecosystems. But for now, a combination of marine no-exploitation zones and programmes aimed at improved marine product management provide the chance for species and ecosystems to become better stabilised.

Artisan fishing at Semporna. The challenge to conserving marine ecosystems is allocating and ensuring use rights in what has to date been an open-access system.

Glossary of Malay/Sabah Words

adat customary law

akasia trees of the genus Acacia, mostly *Acacia mangium* or *A. auriculiformis* in Sabah

Apid-apid *Excoecaria indica*

Aru Casuarina (*Casuarina equisetifolia*)

Auri Tan Wattle (*Acacia auriculiformis*)

Bangkau-bangkau *Borneodendron aenigmaticum*

Belian Borneo Ironwood (*Eusideroxylon zwageri*)

Binuang *Octomeles sumatrana*

bukit hill

Dungun Looking-glass Mangrove (*Heritiera littoralis*)

kapur trees of the genus *Dryobalanops*

kelip-kelip fireflies of the genus *Pteroptyx*

kerangas heath forest

kerapa shallow swamp; the forest found in such areas

keruing trees of the genus *Dipterocarpus*

kota town, city, fort

Laran Kadam, Kadamba (*Anthocephalus chinensis*, also known as *Neolamarckia cadamba*)

Magas *Duabanga moluccana*

Mangium Black Wattle (*Acacia mangium*)

Melawaring Red Sealing-wax Palm (*Cyrtostachys renda*)

Mengaris *Koompassia excelsa*

Mengilan *Agathis borneensis*

Merbau *Intsia palembanica*

Penanga Laut Ballnut (*Calophyllum inophyllum*)

pulau island

Ramin *Gonystylus bancanus*

Seraya Kuning Siput *Shorea faguetiana* and sometimes other *Shorea* trees of the yellow meranti group

taman park

Tembadau Borneo Banteng (*Bos javanicus lowi*)

The Heart of Borneo

The Heart of Borneo is a multinational project co-ordinated by the WWF to conserve 220,000km² of forested highlands in central Borneo.

'Borneo's forests, water and biological diversity are critical for prosperity of the entire island. The continued maintenance of their natural and cultural wealth is of local, national and global importance. At the very heart of Borneo there lies a uniquely rich, largely forested landscape. It straddles the transboundary highlands of Brunei, Indonesia and Malaysia, and reaches out through the foothills into the adjacent lowlands. Our vision for the heart of Borneo is that partnerships at all levels ensure effective management of a network of protected areas, productive forests and other sustainable land-uses. Borneo's magnificent heritage is thereby sustained forever.'

Vision Statement approved by representatives of Brunei, Malaysia and Indonesia at the Heart of Borneo conference in BSB, Brunei Darussalam 1985. www.panda.org, www. wwf.de (Germany), www.wwf.or.id (Indonesia), www.wwf.org.uk (UK), www.wwf.org.my (Malaysia), www.wwf.nl (Netherlands), www. worldwildlife.org (USA).

Bibliography

Argent, G., Lamb, A. and Phillipps, A. (2007). *The Rhododendrons of Sabah, Malaysian Borneo*. Kota Kinabalu: Natural History Publications.

Das, I. and Ghazally, I. (2001). *A Guide to the Lizards of Borneo*. Institute of Biodiversity and Environmental Conservation, Universiti Malaysia Sarawak, website (available at: www.arbec.com.my/lizards).

Garbutt, N. and Prudente, C. (2006). *Wild Borneo. The Wildlife and Scenery of Sabah, Sarawak, Brunei and Kalimantan*. London: New Holland Publishers.

Ghazally, I. and Laily, B.D. (eds) (1995). *A Scientific Journey Through Borneo: Sayap-Kinabalu Park Sabah*. Kuala Lumpur: Pelanduk Publications.

Ghazally, I. and Laily, B.D. (eds) (1995). *A Scientific Journey Through Borneo: Tawau Hill Park Sabah*. Kuala Lumpur: Pelanduk Publications.

Hazebroek, H., Adlin, T.Z.A. and Waidi, S. (2004). *Maliau Basin: Sabah's Lost World*. Kota Kinabalu: Natural History Publications.

Hutton, W. (2008). *Tabin: Sabah's Greatest Wildlife Sanctuary*. Kota Kinabalu: Tabin Wildlife Holidays Sdn. Bhd.

Inger, R.F. and Stuebing, R.B. (2005). *A Field Guide to the Frogs of Borneo*. Kota Kinabalu: Natural History Publications.

Keith, A.N. (2006). *Land Below the Wind*. Kota Kinabalu: Natural History Publications. A reprint of a 1939 classic on life in British North Borneo in the 1930s.

Lim, C.K. and Cranbrook, E. (2002). *Swiftlets of Borneo: Builders of Edible Nests*. Kota Kinabalu: Natural History Publications.

MacKinnon, K., Hatta, G., Hakimah, H. and Mangalik, A. (1997). *The Ecology of Kalimantan, Indonesian Borneo*. Oxford: Oxford University Press. Although out of print and referring largely to Kalimantan, this book contains much ecological information and examples that apply equally to Sabah.

Mann, C.F. (2008). *The Birds of Borneo*. Peterborough: British Ornithologists' Union.

Nais, J. (2001). *Rafflesia of the World*. Kota Kinabalu: Sabah Parks.

Payne, J. and Francis, C. (1985). *A Field Guide to the Mammals of Borneo*. Kota Kinabalu: The Sabah Society.

Payne, J., Cubitt, G. and Lau, D. (1994). *This is Borneo*. London: New Holland Publishers.

Phillipps, A., Lamb, A. and Lee, C.C. (2008). *Pitcher Plants of Borneo*. Kota Kinabalu: Natural History Publications.

Phillipps, Q. and Phillipps, K. (2010). *Phillipps' Field Guide to the Birds of Borneo*. Oxford: John Beaufoy Publishing.

Pio, D. (2005). *Borneo's Lost World. Newly Discovered Species on Borneo*. Jakarta: WWF-Indonesia (available online at: http://assets.panda.org/downloads/newlydiscoveredspeciesonborneo25042005.pdf).

Rautner, M., Hardiono, M. and Alfred, R. (2005). *Borneo: Treasure Island at Risk*. Frankfurt am Main: WWF-Germany (available online at: http://assets.panda.org/downloads/treasureislandatrisk.pdf.

Rowthorn, C., Williams, C. and Cohen, M. (2008). *Borneo*. London: Lonely Planet.

Soepadmo, E., Saw, L.G. and Chung, R.C.K. (eds) (2004). *Tree Flora of Sabah and Sarawak. Volume 5*. Kuala Lumpur: Forest Research Institute Malaysia. This volume, one in a series, contains the most up-to-date and comprehensive treatment of the Dipterocarpaceae.

Stuebing, R. and Inger, R.F. (1999). *A Field Guide to the Snakes of Borneo*. Kota Kinabalu: Natural History Publications.

Treacher, W.H. (1891). *British Borneo: Sketches of Brunai, Sarawak, Labuan and North Borneo*. Singapore: Government Printing Department (available online at: www.gutenberg.org/files/27547/27547-h/27547-h.htm).

Wong, K.M. and Phillipps, A. (eds) (1996). *Kinabalu: Summit of Borneo*. Kota Kinabalu: Natural History Publications.

Wood, J.J. and Cribb, P.J. (1994). *Checklist of the Orchids of Borneo*. Kew, London: Royal Botanic Gardens.

Websites

Danum Valley, www.searrp.org/danum.cfm
Kota Kinabalu City Bird Sanctuary, www.sabahwetlands.org/kkwc/
Land Empowerment Animals People (LEAP), www.leapspiral.org
Martin and Osa Johnson Safari Museum, www.safarimuseum.com/exhib_photo_online.htm (examples of Martin and Osa Johnson's photos of Kinabatangan and Sandakan in 1920 and 1935–36).
Sabah Forestry Department, www.forest.sabah.gov.my
Sabah Parks, www.sabahparks.org.my
The Sabah Society, http://thesabahsociety.com/blog
Sabah Tourism Board, www.sabahtourism.com
Sabah Wildlife Department, www.sabah.gov.my/jhl
Universiti Malaysia Sabah, www.ums.edu.my
WWF-Malaysia, www.wwf.org.my

Acknowledgements

All the people mentioned by name in the text are amongst those who deserve special mention in relation to the issues, species and sites described in this book. All have made major and specific contributions in one way or another towards sustaining the wild species and habitats of wild Sabah.

The following represent some of the many others who have provided support, assistance and information, over many years, that contributed towards conservation of wild Sabah and the contents of this book: Agnes Lee Agama; Dr Marc Ancrenaz, Dr Isabelle Lackman-Ancrenaz and the staff of Kinabatangan Orang-utan Conservation Project; Carol Angkangon Prudente and the staff of North Borneo Safari Sdn. Bhd.; the Chief Minister's Department of the Government of Sabah; Earl of Cranbrook; Darrel Webber; Dr A. Glyn Davies; Dr Geoffrey Davison; Flory Siambun; Dr Charles and Cecilia Francis; Hajjah Hajijah Hamid; Dr Abdul Hamid Ahmad; Hazilah Mohamad; Hazmilah Sulaiman; Gerald Hiu; Ross Ibbotson; Datuk Irene Charuruks and staff of Sabah Tourism Board; Kan Yau Chong; Tan Sri Mohd. Khir Johari; Dato' Dr Mikaail Kavanagh; Lam Ying Fan; the Lasimbang family; Dr Laurentius Ambu and all the staff of Sabah Wildlife Department since 1988; Datuk Lamri Ali and staff of Sabah Parks since 1979; Lonia Adam; Datuk Panglima K.M. Mastan and staff of Sabah Forestry Department since 1979; Matius Sator (as District Officer, Kinabatangan, 1988–94); Adam J. Payne; Melissa J. Payne; Susan, Quentin, Karen, Charles and Anthea Phillipps; Dr Rajanathan and Lynette Rajaratnam; Dr Glen Reynolds; Dato' Dr Dionysius S.K. Sharma, Maria Christina Fung and all the staff of WWF-Malaysia; Saimon Ambi; Justine Vaz; Dr Waidi Sinun and staff of the Yayasan Sabah Group; Dr A. Christy Williams; Datuk Yeo Boon Hai and staff of the Ministry of Tourism and Environmental Development (1988–94); Sylvia Yorath; Stefan Ziegler and staff of WWF-Germany; Wim Ellenbroek and staff of WWF-Netherlands; Wendy Elliott, Diane Walkington and staff of WWF-UK; Tom Dillon and staff of WWF-US. Apologies are extended to those many individuals whose names have been subsumed under the name of their institution and those who have been omitted inadvertently.

Usually, senior politicians are not mentioned in the acknowledgements to books of this nature, but I would like to name five whom I believe have made important and bold decisions that have contributed towards the continuing existence of several wild areas in Sabah. Datuk Mohd Harris Salleh, as Chief Minister in 1984 decided to create a 'permanent forest estate' covering about half Sabah's land area, which to a very large extent remains to this day. With the possible exception of Brunei, no other state or nation in the Asian region made such a decisive and bold decision in the early days of exploitation of natural forests. Without that decision, several of the most significant wildlife conservation areas in Asia might not have existed in Sabah today. In late 1994, Datuk Seri Salleh Said Keruak was instrumental in deciding in favour of the establishment of Kinabatangan Wildlife Sanctuary, which, although a relatively small area, was hotly contested by a large number of interests. Tan Sri Chong Kah Kiat saw this process through to completion. In 2007, Chief Minister Datuk Seri Panglima Musa Haji Aman, as minister for forests, gave his blessing to retention and restoration of Ulu Segama Malua as a forest ecosystem, rather than taking the easier route of conversion to plantations. In recent years, Datuk Masidi Manjun as State Minister of Tourism, Culture and Environment has been an active supporter of many nature conservation initiatives.

The opinions expressed in this book do not necessarily reflect those of any individual or organisation mentioned in the book.

Publisher's Acknowledgements

The publisher would like to express special thanks to Dato' Dr Dionysius S.K. Sharma, Executive Director of WWF-Malaysia, Dato' Seri Tengku Zainal Adlin, Datuk Irene Benggon Charuruks, and Noredah Othman at the Sabah Tourism Board, and Mr Ken Scriven for their help and encouragement during the preparation of this book.

Index

Page references in *italic* refer to photographs.

Abai 92, 110, 177
Abdul Mumin, Sultan 11
Acacia 53, 115, 139
Acacia auriculiformis (Tan
    Wattle) 53
    mangium (Black Wattle) 53
Aceros carnatus (White-
    crowned Hornbill) *184*
    corrugatus (Wrinkled
    Hornbill) 44
adat 110, 112
Adlin, Tengku D.Z. 140
Aerodramus fuciphagus
    (Edible-nest Swiftlet) 167
    maximus (Black-nest
    Swiftlet) 167
Aethopyga mystacalis (Scarlet
    Sunbird) 139
Agathis Camp 142
Agathis trees 46, 140, 142
    borneensis 142
Albizia falcataria 145
Alcedo meninting (Blue-eared
    Kingfisher) *170*
Ambi, Simon 162
Andau, Patrick 75, 193
Anhinga melanogaster (Oriental
    Darter) 170, *170*, 183
Anorrhinus galeritus (Bushy-
    crested Hornbill) 44
Anthocephalus chinensis
    (Laran) 30, 61
Anthracoceros albirostris (Pied
    hornbill) 38
    malayanus (Black Hornbill)
    44
Anthreptes singalensis (Ruby-
    cheeked Sunbird) *69*
Apid-apid tree (*Excoecaria
    indica*) 34
Aplonis panayensis (Asian
    Glossy Starling) *53*, 115
Arachnothera juliae (White-
    head's Spiderhunter) 139
Arachnothera longirostra (Little
    Spiderhunter) *81*
Ardea purpurea (Purple
    Heron) 117, 118
Argusianus argus (Great Argus
    Pheasant) 44, *45*
Aru trees 33, *32–3*, 117, 120,
    123
Avicennia trees *34*

Babbler, Grey-breasted (*Mala-
    copteron albogulare*) 129
Bajau people 103, 130, 148, 161
Bakapit 161
Balambangan, Pulau 121
Ballnut (Penaga Laut) (*Callo-
    phyllum inophyllum*) *33*
bamboo 70, 139
Banggi, Pulau 121
Bangkau-bangkau tree (*Borneo-
    dendron aenigmaticum*) 191
Barbet, Golden-naped (*Merga-
    laima pulcherrima*) *141*
Barratt, James 162
Batu Putih 96, 183
Beaman, John 137

Bear, Sun (Honey Bear)
    (*Helarctos malayanus*) 78,
    79, 164, 189, 202
Beccari, Odoardo 42
beeswax 123, 194
Begahak people 161
begonia 50
Belcher, Capt Edward 120
Belian Camp 142
Belian tree 31, 44
Bengkoka Peninsula 121, 200
Berhala, Pulau *17*, 18, 193,
    198
Bidu-bidu Hills & Forest
    Reserve 121, 191
Binuang (*Octomeles
    sumatrana*) 61
biodiversity, loss of 62–3, 145
birds' nest harvesting 167–8,
    194
Birdwing Butterfly, Rajah
    Brooke's (*Trogonoptera
    brookiana*) *69*
Bisaya people 104
Bittern, Cinnamon (*Ixobrychus
    cinnamomeus*) 118
Biun, Alim 140
Blackeye, Mountain
    (*Chlorocharis emilae*) 139
Bodgaya, Pulau *19*, 20, 146
Boheyduang, Pulau *19*, 20, 146
Bole river 155
Borneodendron aenigmaticum
    (Bangkau-bangkau tree)
    191
Bradypterus accentor (Kinabalu
    Friendly Bush-warbler)
    139
Bristlehead, Bornean (*Pityriasis
    gymnocephalia*) *197*, 198
British North Borneo Company
    106, 110, 122, 159, 187, 194
British North Borneo Herald
    12, 77
Broadbill, Long-tailed
    (*Psarisomus dalhousiae*) 130
    Whitehead's (*Calyptomena
    whiteheadi*) 139
Bruguiera 33
Bubalus bubalus (Water
    Buffalo) 129, 130
Buceros rhinoceros (Rhinoceros
    Hornbill) 44, *71*
Buffalo, Water (*Bubalus
    bubalus*) 129, 130
Bukit Garam 38
Bukit Hampuan 63
Bukit Taviu Forest Reserve 191
Bukit Tengjorak 146
Bukit Wakid *133*
Bulbul, Hook-billed (*Setornis
    criniger*) 129
Burgess, Peter 154
Bush-warbler, Kinabalu
    Friendly (*Bradypterus
    accentor*) 139
Butorides striata (Striated
    Heron) 118
butterflies *69*, 121

Callosciurus notatus (Plantain
    Squirrel) 117
Callophyllum inophyllum
    (Penaga Laut/Ballnut) *33*
Calyptomena whiteheadi (White-
    head's Broadbill) 139

Camphorwood tree (*kapur*)
    27, 28, 42, 190
Carpococcyx radiatus (Bornean
    Ground-cuckoo) *43*, 44
Casuarina equisetifolia (Aru)
    33, *32–3*, 117, 120, *123*
Cat, Bay (*Catopuma badia*) 79,
    153
    Leopard (*Prionailurus
    bengalensis*) *158*, 164
Catopuma badia (Bay Cat) 79,
    153
Cerbera 174–5
Cervus unicolor (Sambar Deer)
    109, 122, 132
Ceyx erithacus (Oriental Dwarf
    Kingfisher) *66*
Chelonia mydas (Green Turtle)
    149, 198, *200*
China 167
Chlorocharis emilae (Mountain
    Blackeye) 139
Christianity 109
Christmas Island 120
Ciconia stormi (Storm's Stork
    169, 170
Civet, Malay (*Viverra
    tanalunga*) *159*
climate and temperatures 12–
    13, 23
climate change 202
Climbathon, Mount Kinabalu
    International 140
climbing 139, 140
coal 18
cocoa plantations 145
Coluga 79, *79*
conservation, development of
    72–5
    land ownership issues 111
    legislation 73
    agencies 74–5
coral 146, 148
Coral Triangle 148, 202
Crake, White-browed
    (*Porzana cinerea*) 118
Crocker, William 133
Crocker Range *19*, 20, 46, 60,
    104, 126, 133–40, 202
Crocodile, Estuarian
    (*Crocodylus porosus*) 35,
    128, 129, *182–3*, 183
crystalline basement rock 15,
    16
customary law (*adat*) 110, 112
Cycad (*Cycas rumphii*) 146
Cyriopagopus thorelli
    (Malaysian Tarantula) *86*
Cyrtostachys renda (Red
    Sealing Wax/Melawaring
    Palm) 129

Dabnum, Mount 191
Dactylocladus stenostachys
    (Jongkong) 129
Danuau Girang 177
Danum Valley 15, 16, 25–6,
    26, 31, 42, 44, *65*, 74, 75,
    99, 152, 154–9, 202
    creation of conservation
    area 154–5
    Field Centre 157–8
Darter, Oriental (*Anhinga
    melanogaster*) 170, *170*, 183
Darvel Bay 12, *12*
Datu Sapindin 12

Davies, Glyn 145
de Silva, Stanley 195
Dendrocitta cinerascens
    (Bornean Treepie) 139
Dent Peninsula 12, 21, *36*, 38,
    159–64, 200
Deer, Red Barking (*Muntiacus
    muntjak*) 44, 132
    Sambar (*Cervus unicolor*)
    109, 122, 132
Deramakot Forest Reserve
    70, 71, 186–9
Dial, Roman 145
Dicerorhinus sumatrensis
    (Sumatran Rhinoceros)
    100
    s. harrisonii (Bornean
    Rhinoceros) 75, 99–
    100, 101, *101*, 189, 202
    Borneo Rhino Sanctuary
    164, 188–9
    conservation of 162–4
Dinochloa 70
Dipterocarps 23, 25, 27–9, *28*,
    30, 31, 42, 44, 68, *76*, 77,
    145, 190
Dipterocarpus lowii 22
Dracaena multiflora 146
Draco cornutus (Flying Lizard)
    83
drought 11, 25, 29–30, 60,
    112, 155, 191, 197
Dryobalanops 27, 28, 42
    aromatica 42
    beccarii (Red Kapur) 42
    keithii 42
    lanceolata 42
    rappa (Swamp Kapur) 42
Duabanga moluccana (Magas) 61
Dungun tree (Looking-glass
    Mangrove) (*Heritiera
    littoralis*) 34
Durian (*Durio zibethinus*) *109*
Dusun people 104, 109, 155

Egret, Little (*Egretta garzetta*)
    118
    Pacific Reef (*Egretta
    sacra*) 117
Eikyo Maru shipwreck 121
El Niño droughts 11, 25, 29–
    30, 60, 112, 155, 191, 197
Elephant, Bornean (*Elaphas
    maximus borneensis*) 18,
    39, 77, *81*, 96–8, 96–9, *152*,
    164, 170, *180–81*, 183, 185,
    189, 202
    Java (*Elephas hysudrindus*)
    99
Elmer, Adolph 193
Eretmochelys imbricata
    (Hawksbill Turtle) 198
Erolia ruficollis (Rufous-
    necked Stint) 118
Eumias indigo (Indigo
    Flycatcher) *84*, 138
Euphorbia lacei (Milk Bush)
    146
Eurycima longifolia (Tongat
    Ali) 109
Eusideroxylon zwageri (Borneo
    Ironwood) 31, 44, 198
Excoecaria indica (Apid-apid
    tree) 34
Exilisciurus exilis (Least
    Pygmy Squirrel) 170

fauna survey report, 1982 75
FELDA 12
Ferret-badger, Bornean
    (*Melogale everetti*) 79
Ficus 38, 51, *51*
Fig, Weeping (*Ficus
    benjamina*) 51
figs, strangling 51
fireflies 34
fishing 107, *108*
Fish-owl, Buffy (*Ketupa
    ketupu*) 170, *172*
floodplain as ecosystem 172–
    7, 185–6
Flowerpecker, Scarlet-
    breasted (*Prionochilus
    thoracicus*) 129
Flycatcher, Asian Paradise
    (*Tersiphone paradisi*) *66*
Flycatcher, Indigo (*Eumias
    indigo*) *84*, 138
flying squirrels 82, 83
Flying Squirrel, Red Giant
    (*Petaurista petaurista*) *83*,
    198
forests:
    age of 27–9
    changing nature of 23–4
    management by local
    communities 112–13
    sustainability 71–2
forest restoration 64–70
    approaches 65
    FACE 68
    INFAPRO 68, 70
    management units 66–7,
    71–3
    restoration methods 68–
    70
    seedling planting 68, 70
Forest Stewardship Council
    (FSC) criteria 189
forest types 25–6
    coastal 31–5
    dipterocarp 27–9, 42, 44,
    59, 76, 77, 145, 189,
    198, 200
    freshwater swamp 37–8
    heath 48–9, 50
    limestone
    mangrove 31–5, 202
    montane 46–7
    palm swamp 35–7
    peat-swamp 39
    riverine 38, 39
    ultrabasic 50–1, 191
Forests Absorbing Carbon
    Dioxide Emissions
    (FACE) Foundation 68
fossils 77, 99
freshwater swamp 37–8
Frigatebird, Christmas Island
    (*Fregata andrewsi*) 120
    Lesser (*Fregata ariel*) 120
fungi 87, *87*, *88*

Galeopterus variegatus (Sunda
    Flying Lemur) 79, *79*, 82,
    82
Garullax palliatus (Sunda
    Laughingthrush) *138*
    mitratus (Chestnut-capped
    Laughingthrush) 139
Gasis, Joseph 143
Gaya, Pulau 111–20
geology 15–21

German Agency for Technical Co-operation (GTZ) 189
Gibbon, Bornean (*Hylobates muelleri*) 24, 44, 90, *92*, 130
Gibbs, Lilian 137
Gigantochloa levis (Bamboo) 139
Glyphotes simus (Red-bellied Sculptor Squirrel) 143
Gomantong hill 50, *165–6*, 167–9, *167*, 183
Gonystylus bancanus (Ramin) 129
Grand Devil's Claw (*Pisonia grandis*) 120
Ground-cuckoo, Bornean (*Carpococcyx radiatus*) *43*, 44, 170
Gunung Lotung 75
Gymnostoma nobile (Sempilau Laut) 129

Halcyon copensis (Stork-billed Kingfisher) *128*, 129
Haliaeetus leucogaster (White-bellied Sea Eagle) 117, *118*
Harpactes diardii (Diard's Trogon) 155
    kasumba (Red-naped Trogon) *84*
    Whiteheadi (Whitehead's Trogon) 139
Harrisson, Tom & Barbara 164, 195
Hatton, Frank 159, 187
    Joseph 11
Hatton, Mount 159, 202
Hawk, Bat (*Macheiramphus alcinus*) 168, 169
Heart of Borneo programme 186, 203
Helarctos malayanus (Sun Bear) 78, 79, 164, 189, 202
Heliastur indus (Brahminy Kite) 117
Heritiera littoralis (Dungun/Looking-glass Mangrove) 34
Heron, Purple (*Ardea purpurea*) 117, 118
    Striated (*Butorides striata*) 118
Hevea brasiliensis (Para Rubber) 139
Himantopus himantopus (Black-winged Stilt) 118
honey 123, 194
hornbills 143, 185
    Black (*Anthracoceros malayanus*) 44
    Bushy-crested (*Anorrhinus galeritus*) 44
    Helmeted (*Rhinoplax vigil*) 44, 85
    Oriental Pied (*Anthracoceros albirostris*) 38
    Rhinoceros (*Buceros rhinoceros*) 44, 71
    White-crowned (*Aceros carnatus*) *184*
    Wrinkled (*Aceros corrugatus*) 44
Hunt, John 11, 194
hunting and trapping 108–9, 132

hydroelectric power 72
Hylobates muelleri (Bornean Gibbon) 24, 44, 90, *92*, 130

Ibul 132
Idahan people 109, 169
Imbak Canyon & river 189–90, *191*, 202
indigenous society:
    clothing 103
    diet 104, 107–9
    egalitarian nature of 106
    forest management 112–13
    housing *103*, 103
    hunting 108–9, 132
    land ownership 106–7, 110–12
    religion 109
INFRAPRO 68, 158
Inger, Dr 188
International Union for Conservation of Nature and Natural Resources (IUCN) 163
Intsia palembanica (Merbau) 44
invertebrates, food sources 80, 86–7
Iranun people 130
Ironwood, Borneo (Belian) (*Eusideroxylon zwageri*) 31, 44, 198
Islam 109
Ixobrychus cinnamomeus (Cinnamon Bittern) 118

Johnson, Martin & Osa 96
Jongkong (*Dactylocladus stenostachys*) 129

Kadazan-Dusun people 109
Kalampunian, Pulau 120
Kalimantan 104, 105
Kampung Hindian Forest Reserve 129
Kampung Kituau 136
kapur (Camphorwood) 27, 28, 42
    Red 42, 190
    Swamp 42
Keith, Agnes 161
    Harry 42
Kelip-kelip 34
Keningau 21, 135, 141
kerangas 48, 63
kerapa 49
Keruing 44
Ketanun Valley 132
Ketupa ketupu (Buffy Fish-owl) 170, *172*
Kiau 140
Kinabalu, Mount 16, 19, *19*, 20, 23, 29, 46, 47, 63, 104, 130, 133, 136–40, 187, 191
Kinabatangan River & Plain 17, 34, 37, *37*, 38, 39, *49*, 92, 96, 99, 110, *111*, 152, 169–86, 187, 202
    conservation work in 177–86
    significance 172–7
    wildlife in 169–70
Kinabatangan Wildlife Sanctuary 74, 183–6
Kingfisher, Banded (*Lacedo pulchella*) 155
    Blue-eared (*Alcedo meninting*) 170

Oriental Dwarf (*Ceyx erithacus*) 66
    Stork-billed (*Halcyon copensis*) *128*, 129
Kite, Brahminy (*Heliastur indus*) 117
Klias Peninsula & Reserve 21, 33, 39, 42, 60, 63, 120, 126–9
Koompassia excelsa (Mengaris) *43*, 44, 126
Kota Belud 121, 129
Kota Kinabalu *8*, 19, 30, 34, 115–18 136
    Bird Sanctuary *116*, 117
Kota Morudu 123
Kuala Penyu 120, 127
Kudat Peninsula 123–5, *122–3*, *124–5*
Kulamba Wildlife Reserve 21, *32*, 38, *61*, 75, 200–1

Labuk River & Valley 16, 18, 37, 164, 187
Lacedo pulchella (Banded Kingfisher) 155
Lahad Datu 109, 136, 152–64, 191
Lalage nigra (Pied Triller) 117
Lamb, Tony 141
land capability classification mapping, 1976 74
Land Ordinance 1930 73, 106, 112
land ownership 72, 106, 110–12
land snails 50
langurs *see* leaf monkeys
Laran (Kadam) (*Anthocephalus chinensis*) 30, 61
Laticauda colubrine (Yellow-lipped Sea Krait) 118
Laughingthrush, Chestnut-capped (*Garrulax mitratus*) 139
    Sunda (*Garrulax palliatus*) 138
laurel 46
leaf monkeys (langurs) 35, 44, 80, 92
    Grey (Hose's) (*Presbytis hosei*) 92, *93*
    Red (*Presbytis rubicunda*) 44, *80*, 92, 130, *130*, 144, *144*, 153
    Silver (*Tracypithecus cristatus*) 35, 92, 129
Lemur, Sunda Flying (Coluga) (*Galeopterus variegatus*) 79, *79*, 82, *82*
Leong, K.M. 154
Leopard, Bornean Clouded (*Neofelis diardi*) 78, 164, 189, 202
lianas 52
Libaran, Pulau 198
Likas Lagoon 118
limestone 19, 50, 164–9
Lingham, Wilfred 183
Linumunsut, Lake 142
Lizard, Flying (*Draco cornutus*) 83
logging industry 54–63, 66, 141
    & biodiversity 62–3
    development of 54–7
    logged forests, characteristics of 59–61

'log ponds' 194
'reduced impact' experiments 159
    & sustainability 71, 75, 189
Lokan peneplain 187–8, 194
Long Mio 132
Long Pasia 132
Lophura bulweri (Bulwer's Pheasant) 143
Loris, Borneo Slow (*Nycticebu coucang menagensis*) 95
Low, Sir Hugh 11, 139
Lower Kinabatangan-Segama Wetlands 200
Lumerau Commercial Forest Reserve 163
Lumnitzera 34
Lun Dayeh people 104, 130, 132

macaques 109
    Long-tailed (*Macaca fascicularis*) 35, *35*, 92, 129
    Pig-nosed (*Macaca nemestrina*) 92, *94*
Macaranga 30, 61
Macheiramphus alcinus (Bat Hawk) 168, 169
Macrobachrium rosenburgii (giant freshwater prawn) 108
Madai 19, 169
Madalon, Mount 140
Magas (*Duabanga moluccana*) 61
Magdalena, Mount 143
Mahua waterfall *134–5*
malaria 109
Malaysia, land tenure in 111–12
Maliau Basin 17–18, 44, 46, *46*, 48–9, *50*, 140, 141–3, 202
Maliau Falls 18, 142, *142*
Malacopteron albogulare (Grey-breasted Babbler) 129
Maligan 132
Malkoha, Raffles's (*Phaenicophaeus chlorophaeus*) 132
Mallotus muticus (Swamp Mallotus) *184*, 185
Malua 72, 152
    BioBank 159
mammals, diet 77–8
Mamutik, Pulau *119*, 120
Mangrove trees & forest 33–5, *174–5*, 200–1, 202
    Looking-glass Mangrove (*Heritiera littoralis*) 34
Mannan, Sam 64
Mantanai, Pulau 121
Manukan, Pulau *119*, 120
Marsh, Dr Clive 155, 156
Marudu Bay 121, 123
Megapodus cumingii (Tabon Scrubfowl) 121
Melapi 169, 183
Melogale everetti (Bornean Ferret-badger) 79
Menanggul River & Forest 64, 169, 183
Mengalum, Pulau 120–21
Mengaris (*Koompassia excelsa*) *43*, 44, 126
Merbau (*Intsia palembanica*) 44

Mergalaima pulcherrima (Golden-naped Barbet) 141
Milk Bush (*Euphorbia lacei*) 146
Monkey, Proboscis (*Nasalis larvatus*) 35, 38, 94–5, *95*, 129, 129, 170, 183
Mousedeer, Lesser (*Tragulus javanicus*) 158
mud volcanoes 18, 20, 76, 120, 164
mudskippers (*Periothalamus*) *127*, 129
Munang, Miller 189
Muntiacus muntjak (Red Barking Deer) 44, *132*
Murut people *102*, 103, 109, 130, 132
Musa borneensis 142

Nabahan Forest Reserve 129
Nabawan 49, 63
Nasalis larvatus (Proboscis Monkey) 35, 38, 94–5, *95*, 129, *129*, 170, 183
Nathan, Dr Sen 164
native title 112
nature tourism 11, 111, 183, 196–8
Nectarinia jugularis (Olive-backed Sunbird) 144
Neofelis diardi (Bornean Clouded Leopard) 78, 164, 189, 202
Nepenthes 46, 47, 49, 53, *53*
    ampullaria 53
    rajah 47
    veitchii 49
New England Power Company, USA 158
Nibong forest 35–7, *36*
Nibong Palm (*Oncosperma tigillarium*) 35–7, *36*, 174–5
Nipah Palm (*Nypa fruticans*) 35, 36, 129, 174–5, 200
Nycticebu coucang menagensis (Bornean Slow Loris) 95

oak 46, 139
Oban people 161
Octomeles sumatrana (Binuang) 61
oil palm plantation 62, 71, 74, 96, 111, 172, 186, 188
Oncosperma tigillarium (Nibong Palm) 35–7, *36*, 174–5
Ong, Cynthia 111
Ong, Dr Robert 64
Orang Sungai people *107*, 172, 183
Orang-utan, Bornean (*Pongo pygmaeus*) 29, 30, 35, 39, 44, 63, 71, 72, 75, 90, *91*, 53, 185, 189, 200, 202
    Rehabilitation Centre, Sepilok 193, 195–8
orchid 50, 52, 77, 90, *91*, 138, 145, 170, 183
    Moon (*Phalaenopsis amabilis*) 52
    slipper (*Paphiopedilum lowii*) 52
    slipper (*Paphiopedilum rothschildianum*) 138
Renthera bella 138

Orthotomus cuclatus (Mountain Tailorbird) 139
Otus mantananensis (Mantanani Scops Owl) 121
Owl, Mantanani Scops (*Otus mantanensis*) 121
oxbow lakes 38, *40–41*, 173, 177

Padang Teratak 129
Padas river & gorge 37, 104, 126–7, 135, 141
Paitan river 60, 123, 130
palm-swamp forest 35–7
palms 35–7, 52
  Nibong Palm (*Oncosperma tigillarium*) 35–7, *36*, *174–5*
  Nipah Palm (*Nypa fructicans*) 35, *36* 129, *174–5*, 200
  rattans 52
  Red Sealing Wax (Melawaring) Palm (*Cyrtostachys renda*) 129
Paloh, Yuya 156
Panar Laban 140
paper making 132–3
Paphiopedilum javanicum var. *virens* 52
  rothschildianum *138*
Parashorea tomentella 30
Parrot, Blue-naped (*Tanygnathus lucionensis*) 117
peat swamps 39, 127, 129
Pelian (*Tor tambroides*) *108*
Penaga Laut (Ballnut) (*Callophyllum inophyllum*) 33
Periothalamus 127, 129
Phaenicophaeus chlorophaeus (Raffles's Malkoha) *132*
Phalaenopsis amabilis (Moon Orchid) 52
Pheasant, Bulwer's (*Lophura bulweri*) 143
  Great Argus (*Argusianus argus*) 44, *45*
Phyllocladus 46
Pig, Bearded (*Sus barbatus*) 44, 78, *78*, 109, 164, 188
pigs, domestic 107–8
Pinosuk plateau 27, 29
Pisonia grandis (Grand Devil's-claws tree) 120
pitcher plant (*Nepenthes*) 46, *47*, *49*, 53
Pitta, Banded (*Pitta guajana*) 136
  Black and Crimson (*Pitta ussheri*) 161
  Blue-headed (*Pitta baudii*) 145
  Blue-winged (*Pitta moluccensis*) 136
  Hooded (*Pitta sordida*) 182
Plasmodium knowlesi 109
Pock, Mount 19
Podocarpus 46
Pongo pygmaeus (Bornean Orang-utan) 29, 30, 35, 39, 44, 63, 71, 72, 75, 77, 153, 185, 189, 200, 202
  pygmaeus morio 90
Poring 44, 139
Porzana cinerea (White-browed Crake) 118

prawns, giant freshwater (*Macrobachrium rosenburgii*) 108
Presbytis hosei (Grey (Hose's) Leaf Monkey) 92, *93*
Prionailurus bengalensis (Leopard Cat) *158*, 164
Prionochilus thoracicus (Scarlet-breasted Flowerpecker) 129
primates 90–6
Protection of Forests in Europe, Conference on, 1993 57
Pryer, William 12, 187, 194
Psarisomus dalhousiae (Long-tailed Broadbill) 130
Pterospermum 61
Pulau Tiga Park 120
Pityriasis gymnocephalia (Bornean Bristlehead) *197*, 198
Python reticulates (Reticulated Python) *80*

Rafflesia 44, 53, 139, 140
  keithii *45*, *140*, 141
  pricei 135
  tengku-adlinii 140
  tetrastigma 53, 141
Rafflesia Forest Reserve 135, 143
rainfall distribution 12
Rainforest Discovery Centre, Sepilok *74–5*, 198
Ramin (*Gonystylus bancanus*) 129
Ramos, Maximo 193
Ramsar Convention 200
rattans 52
Reinwardtipicus validus (Orange-backed Woodpecker) *85*
Renanthera bella 138
Rhinoceros, Bornean (*Dicerorhinus sumatrensis harrisonii*) 75, 99–101, *100*, *101*, 189, 202
  Borneo Rhino Sanctuary 164, 188–9
  conservation of 162–4
  Java (*Rhinoceros sondaicus*) 77, 202
  Sumatran (Asian Two-horned) (*Dicerorhinus sumatrensis*) 100
Rhinoplax vigil (Helmeted Hornbill) 44, 85
Rhizophora 33, *34*
rice growing 104–5, 172–3
Royal Society, UK 158
roads 112, 132
Rungu people 103, 123, 126

Sabah, origins of name 11–12
Sabah Forestry Department 66, *73*, 74, 75, 123, 155, 162, 185, 189
Sabah Foundation 26, 56, 64, 66, 74, 123, 155, 158, 189
Sabah Wildlife Department 74, 164, 183, 185
Sabahan river 11–12
Saburi, Rashid 162
Sahabat 12

Sandakan 17, 18, 30, *73*, 187, *192*, 193–4, 200
  Rainforest Park 193
Sandpiper, Wood (*Tringa glareola*) 118
sandstones 17–18
Sapi, Pulau 120
Scriven, Ken 155
Scrubfowl, Tabon (*Megapodus cumingii*) 121
Sea Eagle, White-bellied (*Haliaeetus leucogaster*) 117, *118*
Sea Krait, Yellow-lipped (*Laticauda colubrine*) 120
sea snakes 120
sedimentary rocks 17–18
Segaliud-Lokan 189
Segama river 16, 26, 37, 99, 155, 156, 159, 162
Selingan *199*, *201*
Sempilau Laut (*Gymnostoma nobile*) 129
Semporna Peninsula 16, 20, 146–51
Sepilok 31, 42, 48, *74*, 156, 193, 194–8, 202
  Orang-utan Rehabilitation Centre 193, 195–8
Seraya Kuning Siput (*Shorea figuetiana*) 42, 145
Setornis criniger (Hook-billed Bulbul) 129
Sharaf ud-Din, Sultan 194
shipwrecks 121
Shorea figuetiana (Seraya Kuning Siput) 42, 145
  superba 31
Silabukan Commercial Forest Reserve 162, 163
Silam, Mount 12, 16, 191
Silimpopon 18
Sinun, Dr Wadi 99
Sipadan, Pulau 148
Sipitang 130, 132
slipper orchids *52*, *138*
soils 21, 25
Sook plain 21, 30
South China Sea Islands 118–21
Spiderhunter, Little (*Arachnothera longirostra*) *81*
  Whitehead's (*Arachnothera juliae*) 139
squirrels 143
  Least Pygmy (*Exilisciurus exilis*) 170
  Plantain (*Calliosciurus notatus*) 117
  Red-bellied Sculptor (*Glyphotes simus*) 143
St John, Spenser 19
  Life in the Forests of the Far East 96
Starling, Asian Glossy (*Aplonis panayensis*) 53, 115
State Reserves 72–5
Stawin, Herman 164
Stilt, Black-winged (*Himantopus himantopus*) 118
Stint, Rufous-necked (*Erolia ruficollis*) 118
Stork, Storm's (*Ciconia stormi*) *169*, 170
Sugud Recreation Forest 136

Sugut Islands Marine Conservation Area (SIMCA) 198–9
Sugut river 37, 39, 60, 123
Sukau *49*, *111*, 169, 177, 183
Sulu Sea 202
Sulu Sultanate 123, 148, 183, 194
Sulug, Pulau *119*, 120
Suluk people 148, 161
Sunbird, Olive-backed (*Nectarinia jugularis*) 144
  Ruby-cheeked (*Anthreptes singalensis*) 69
  Scarlet (*Aethopyga mystacalis*) 139
Sunda Shelf 118
Sundaland 15, 28
Sus barbatus (Bearded Pig) 44, 78, *78*, 109, 164, 188
Swamp Mallotus (*Mallotus muticus*) *184*, 185
swidden farming 104–6
swiflets (*Aerodramus*) 164–9
  Black-nest (*Aerodramus maximus*) 167
  Edible-nest (*Aerodramus fuciphagus*) 167
  nest gathering 167–8, 194

Tabin river 159, *160–1*, 164
Tabin Wildlife Reserve 12, *20*, 75, *76*, 77, 78, 99, 159–64, 202
Tailorbird, Mountain (*Orthotomus cuclatus*) 139
Tambunan 21 137, 140
Tambuyukon, Mount 137
Tangkulap Forest Reserve 189
Tanjung Aru 117
Tanjung Linsang 200
Tanjung Simpang Mengayau 121
tannin 33
Tanygnathus lucionensis (Blue-naped Parrot) 117
Tapir, Malayan (*Tapirus indicus*) 77, 202
Tarantula, Malaysian (*Cyriopagopus thorelli*) *86*
Tarsier, Western (*Tarsius bancanus*) 79, *79*, 95, 198
Tattler, Grey-tailed (*Tringa brevipes*) 118
Tawai Forest Reserve 22, 191
Tawau Hills *19*, 20, 29, 42, 44, 46, 74, 136, 143–5, 202
Tawau river 26
teak trade 123
Telupid 16, 187, 191
Tembadau 122, 142, 189, 201, 202
Tempasuk Plain 121, 123, 129–30
Tenegang Besar river 177
Tenom 20, 21, 137, 141
Tersiphone paradisi (Asian Paradise Flycatcher) *66*
Thalasseus bergii (Great Crested Tern) 120
Thrush, Borneo Island (*Turdus poliocephalus seebohmi*) 139
Tiger (*Panthera tigris*) 77

Tomanggong 161, 162
Tongat Ali (*Eurycima longifolia*) 109
Tor tambroides (Pelian) 108
Tracypithecus cristatus (Silver Leaf Monkey) 35, 92, 129
Tragulus javanicus (Lesser Mousedeer) *158*
Treepie, Bornean (*Dendrocitta cinerascens*) 139
Trema 61
Tridacna 146–7
Triller, Pied (*Lalage nigra*) 117
Tringa brevipes (Grey-tailed Tattler) 118
  glareola (Wood Sandpiper) 118
Trogon, Diard's (*Harpactes diardii*) *155*
  Red-naped (*Harpactes kasumba*) 84
  Whitehead's (*Harpactes Whiteheadi*) 139
Trogonoptera brookiana (Rajah Brooke's Birdwing Butterfly) 69
Trus Madi *133*, 140
Tun Sakaran Marine Park 146
Tungku river 161
Tunku Abdul Rahman Park 115–16, 118–20, *119*
Turdus poliocephalus seebohmi (Borneo Island Thrush) 139
Turtle Islands 74, 193, 198
Turtle, Green (*Chelonia mydas*) 149, 198, 200
  Hawksbill (*Eretmochelys imbricata*) 198

Ulu Padas 130–3
Ulu Sapa Payau Forest Reserve 42
Ulu Segama 13, *60*, *65*, 68, 70, 72, 99, 152–3, 158–9, 191
urban areas 115–18

Vatica 38
vertebrates, small, food sources of 78–9
Viverra tanalunga (Malay Civet) *159*
volcanic activity 19–20

Walsh, Rory 29, 30
Wattle, Black (*Acacia mangium*) 53
  Tan (*Acacia auriculifirmis*) 53
Wenk, Eduard 77, 159
White-eye, Black-capped (*Zosterops atricapillus*) 139
Whitehead, John 139
whitewater rafting 135
Whittaker, Dr Romulus 155
Wong Siew Te 78
Woodpecker, Orange-backed (*Reinwardtipicus validus*) *85*
World War II death marches 187–8, 191
WWF-Malaysia 75, 143, 153, 155, 163

Zosterops atricapillus (Black-capped White-eye) 139